MASTER THE™ DSST

Ethics in America Exam

About Peterson's

Peterson's® has been your trusted educational publisher for over 50 years. It's a milestone we're quite proud of, as we continue to offer the most accurate, dependable, high-quality educational content in the field, providing you with everything you need to succeed. No matter where you are on your academic or professional path, you can rely on Peterson's for its books, online information, expert test-prep tools, the most up-to-date education exploration data, and the highest quality career success resources—everything you need to achieve your education goals. For our complete line of products, visit www.petersons.com.

For more information, contact Peterson's, 8740 Lucent Blvd., Suite 400, Highlands Ranch, CO 80129; 800-338-3282 Ext. 54229; or find us online at **www.petersons.com**.

ISBN: 978-0-7689-4445-7

Printed in the United States of America

10 9 8 7 6 5 4 3 2 1   22   21   20

Contents

Before You Begin

HOW THIS BOOK IS ORGANIZED

Peterson's *Master the™ DSST Ethics in America Exam* provides a diagnostic test, subject-matter review, and a post-test.

- **Diagnostic Test**—Twenty multiple-choice questions, followed by an answer key with detailed answer explanations
- **Assessment Grid**—A chart designed to help you identify areas that you need to focus on based on your test results
- **Subject-Matter Review**—General overview of the exam subject, followed by a review of the relevant topics and terminology covered on the exam.
- **Post-test**—Sixty multiple-choice questions, followed by an answer key and detailed answer explanations

The purpose of the diagnostic test is to help you figure out what you know—or don't know. The twenty multiple-choice questions are similar to the ones found on the DSST exam, and they should provide you with a good idea of what to expect. Once you take the diagnostic test, check your answers to see how you did. Included with each correct answer is a brief explanation regarding why a specific answer is correct, and in many cases, why other options are incorrect. Use the assessment grid to identify the questions you miss so that you can spend more time reviewing that information later. As with any exam, knowing your weak spots greatly improves your chances of success.

Following the diagnostic test is a subject-matter review. The review summarizes the various topics covered on the DSST exam. Key terms are defined; important concepts are explained; and when appropriate, examples are provided. As you read the review, some of the information may seem familiar while other information may seem foreign. Again, take note of the unfamiliar because that will most likely cause you problems on the actual exam.

After studying the subject-matter review, you should be ready for the post-test. The post-test contains sixty multiple-choice items, and it will serve as a dry run for the real DSST exam. There are complete answer explanations at the end of the test.

OTHER DSST® PRODUCTS BY PETERSON'S

Books, flashcards, practice tests, and videos available online at
www.petersons.com/testprep/dsst

- Art of the Western World
- Astronomy
- Business Mathematics
- Business Ethics in Society
- Civil War and Reconstruction
- Computing and Information Technology
- Criminal Justice
- Environmental Science
- Ethics in America
- Ethics in Technology
- Foundations in Education
- Fundamentals of Cybersecurity
- General Anthropology
- Health and Human Development
- History of the Soviet Union
- History of the Vietnam War
- Human Resource Management
- Introduction to Business
- Introduction to Geography
- Introduction to Law Enforcement
- Introduction to World Religions
- Lifespan Developmental Psychology
- Math for Liberal Arts
- Management Information Systems
- Money and Banking
- Organizational Behavior
- Personal Finance
- Introduction to Geology
- Principles of Advanced English Composition
- Principles of Finance
- Principles of Public Speaking
- Principles Statistics
- Principles of Supervision
- Substance Abuse
- Technical Writing

Like what you see? Get unlimited access to Peterson's full catalog of DSST practice tests, instructional videos, flashcards and more for **75% off the first month!** Go to **www.petersons.com/testprep/dsst** and use coupon code **DSST2020** at checkout. Offer expires July 1, 2021.

Chapter 1

All About the DSST® Exam

WHAT IS DSST®?

Previously known as the DANTES Subject Standardized Tests, the DSST program provides the opportunity for individuals to earn college credit for what they have learned outside of the traditional classroom. Accepted or administered at more than 1,900 colleges and universities nationwide and approved by the American Council on Education (ACE), the DSST program enables individuals to use the knowledge they have acquired outside the classroom to accomplish their educational and professional goals.

WHY TAKE A DSST® EXAM?

DSST exams offer a way for you to save both time and money in your quest for a college education. Why enroll in a college course in a subject you already understand? For more than 30 years, the DSST program has offered the perfect solution for people who are knowledgeable in a specific subject and want to save both time and money. A passing score on a DSST exam provides physical evidence to universities of proficiency in a specific subject. More than 1,900 accredited and respected colleges and universities across the nation award undergraduate credit for passing scores on DSST exams. With the DSST program, individuals can shave months off the time it takes to earn a degree.

The DSST program offers numerous advantages for individuals in all stages of their educational development:

- Adult learners
- College students
- Military personnel

1

Adult learners desiring college degrees face unique circumstances—demanding work schedules, family responsibilities, and tight budgets. Yet adult learners also have years of valuable work experience that may be applied toward a degree through the DSST program. For example, adult learners with on-the-job experience in business and management might be able to skip the Business 101 courses if they earn passing marks on DSST exams such as Introduction to Business and Principles of Supervision.

Adult learners can put their prior learning into action and move forward with more advanced course work. Adults who have never enrolled in a college course may feel a little uncertain about their abilities. If this describes your situation, then sign up for a DSST exam and see how you do. A passing score may be the boost you need to realize your dream of earning a degree. With family and work commitments, adult learners often feel they lack the time to attend college. The DSST program provides adult learners with the unique opportunity to work toward college degrees without the time constraints of semester-long course work. DSST exams take two hours or less to complete. In one weekend, you could earn credit for multiple college courses.

The DSST exams also benefit students who are already enrolled in a college or university. With college tuition costs on the rise, most students face financial challenges. The fee for each DSST exam starts at $80 (plus administration fees charged by some testing facilities)—significantly less than the $750 average cost of a 3-hour college class. Maximize tuition assistance by taking DSST exams for introductory or mandatory course work. Once you earn a passing score on a DSST exam, you are free to move on to higher-level course work in that subject matter, take desired electives, or focus on courses in a chosen major.

Not only do college students and adult learners profit from DSST exams, but military personnel reap the benefits as well. If you are a member of the armed services at home or abroad, you can initiate your post-military career by taking DSST exams in areas with which you have experience. Military personnel can gain credit anywhere in the world, thanks to the fact that almost all the tests are available through the internet at designated testing locations. DSST testing facilities are located at more than 500 military installations, so service members on active duty can get a jump-start on a post-military career with the DSST program. As an additional incentive, DANTES (Defense Activity for Non-Traditional Education Support) provides funding for DSST test fees for eligible members of the military.

More than 30 subject-matter tests are available in the fields of Business, Humanities, Math, Physical Science, Social Sciences, and Technology.

Available DSST® Exams

Business	Social Sciences
Business Ethics and Society	A History of the Vietnam War
Business Mathematics	Art of the Western World
Computing and Information Technology	Criminal Justice
Human Resource Management	Foundations of Education
Introduction to Business	Fundamentals of Counseling
Management Information Systems	General Anthropology
Money and Banking	History of the Soviet Union
Organizational Behavior	Introduction to Geography
Personal Finance	Introduction to Law Enforcement
Principles of Finance	Lifespan Developmental Psychology
Principles of Supervision	Substance Abuse
	The Civil War and Reconstruction

Humanities	Physical Science
Ethics in America	Astronomy
Introduction to World Religions	Environmental Science
Principles of Advanced English	Health and Human Development
Composition	Introduction to Geology
Principles of Public Speaking	

Math	Technology
Fundamentals of College Algebra	Ethics in Technology
Math for Liberal Arts	Fundamentals of Cybersecurity
Principles of Statistics	Technical Writing

As you can see from the table, the DSST program covers a wide variety of subjects. However, it is important to ask two questions before registering for a DSST exam.

1. Which universities or colleges award credit for passing DSST exams?
2. Which DSST exams are the most relevant to my desired degree and my experience?

Knowing which universities offer DSST credit is important. In all likelihood, a college in your area awards credit for DSST exams, but find out before taking an exam by contacting the university directly. Then review the list of DSST exams to determine which ones are most relevant to the degree you are seeking and to your base of knowledge. Schedule an appointment with your college adviser to determine which exams best fit your degree program and which college courses the DSST exams can replace. Advisers should also be able to tell you the minimum score required on the DSST exam to receive university credit.

DSST® TEST CENTERS

You can find DSST testing locations in community colleges and universities across the country. Check the DSST website (**www.getcollegecredit. com**) for a location near you or contact your local college or university to find out if the school administers DSST exams. Keep in mind that some universities and colleges administer DSST exams only to enrolled students. DSST testing is available to men and women in the armed services at more than 500 military installations around the world.

HOW TO REGISTER FOR A DSST® EXAM

Once you have located a nearby DSST testing facility, you need to contact the testing center to find out the exam administration schedule. Many centers are set up to administer tests via the internet, while others use printed materials. Almost all DSST exams are available as online tests, but the method used depends on the testing center. The cost for each DSST exam starts at $80, and many testing locations charge a fee to cover their costs for administering the tests. Credit cards are the only accepted payment method for taking online DSST exams. Credit card, certified check, and money order are acceptable payment methods for paper-and-pencil tests.

Test takers are allotted two score reports—one mailed to them and another mailed to a designated college or university, if requested. Online tests generate unofficial scores at the end of the test session, while individuals taking paper tests must wait four to six weeks for score reports.

PREPARING FOR A DSST® EXAM

Even though you are knowledgeable in a certain subject matter, you should still prepare for the test to ensure you achieve the highest score possible. The first step in studying for a DSST exam is to find out what will be on the specific test you have chosen. Information regarding test content is located on the DSST fact sheets, which can be downloaded at no cost from **www. getcollegecredit.com**. Each fact sheet outlines the topics covered on a subject-matter test, as well as the approximate percentage assigned to each topic. For example, questions on the Principles of Supervision exam are distributed in the following way: 20 percent on the roles and responsibilities of the supervisor, 30 percent on organizational environment, and 50 percent on management functions.

In addition to the breakdown of topics on a DSST exam, the fact sheet also lists recommended reference materials. If you do not own the recommended books, then check college bookstores. Avoid paying high prices for new textbooks by looking online for used textbooks. Don't panic if you are unable to locate a specific textbook listed on the fact sheet; the textbooks are merely recommendations. Instead, search for comparable books used in university courses on the specific subject. Current editions are ideal, and it is a good idea to use at least two references when studying for a DSST exam. Of course, the subject matter provided in this book will be a sufficient review for most test takers. However, if you need additional information, it is a good idea to have some of the reference materials at your disposal when preparing for a DSST exam.

Fact sheets include other useful information in addition to a list of reference materials and topics. Each fact sheet includes subject-specific sample questions like those you will encounter on the DSST exam. The sample questions provide an idea of the types of questions you can expect on the exam. Test questions are multiple-choice with one correct answer and three incorrect choices.

The fact sheet also includes information about the number of credit hours ACE has recommended be awarded by colleges for a passing DSST exam score. However, you should keep in mind that not all universities and colleges adhere to the ACE recommendation for DSST credit hours. Some institutions require DSST exam scores higher than the minimum score recommended by ACE. Once you have acquired appropriate reference materials and you have the outline provided on the fact sheet, you are ready to start studying, which is where this book can help.

TEST DAY

After reviewing the material and taking practice tests, you are finally ready to take your DSST exam. Follow these tips for a successful test day experience.

1. **Arrive on time.** Not only is it courteous to arrive on time to the DSST testing facility, but it also allows plenty of time for you to take care of check-in procedures and settle into your surroundings.

2. **Bring identification.** DSST test facilities require that candidates bring a valid government-issued identification card with a current photo and signature. Acceptable forms of identification include a current driver's license, passport, military identification card, or state-issued identification card. Individuals who fail to bring proper identification to the DSST testing facility will not be allowed to take an exam.

3. **Bring the right supplies.** If your exam requires the use of a calculator, you may bring a calculator that meets the specifications. For paper-based exams, you may also bring No. 2 pencils with an eraser and black ballpoint pens. Regardless of the exam methodology, you are NOT allowed to bring reference or study materials, scratch paper, or electronics such as cell phones, personal handheld devices, cameras, alarm wrist watches, or tape recorders to the testing center.

4. **Take the test.** During the exam, take the time to read each question and the provided answers carefully. Eliminate the choices you know are incorrect to narrow the number of potential answers. If a question completely stumps you, take an educated guess and move on—remember that DSSTs are timed; you will have 2 hours to take the exam.

With the proper preparation, DSST exams will save you both time and money. So join the thousands of people who have already reaped the benefits of DSST exams and move closer than ever to your college degree.

ETHICS IN AMERICA EXAM FACTS

The DSST Ethics in America exam was developed to enable schools to award credit to students for knowledge equivalent to that learned by students taking the course. The DSST Ethics in America exam consists of 100 multiple-choice questions to be answered in 2 hours. The exam covers contemporary foundational ethics issues such as relativism, subjectivism, determinism and free will; relationships between morality and religious traditions; the development of ethical traditions from Greeks to modern philosophers; and ethical analysis of various issues such as war, capital punishment, human rights, racism and affirmative action, biomedical ethics, and economic inequity. Critical thinking and logical analysis will be as important as your knowledge of ethical concepts and theories.

Area or Course Equivalent: Ethics in America
Level: Lower-level baccalaureate
Amount of Credit: 3 Semester Hours
Minimum Score: 400
Source: https://www.getcollegecredit.com/wp-content/assets/factsheets/EthicsInAmerica.pdf

Below is an outline of what you can expect to be covered on the exam.

I. Contemporary Foundational Issues – 15%

   a. Relativism

   b. Subjectivism

   c. Determinism and Free Will

   d. Relationship between morality and religion

II. Ethical Traditions – 35%

   a. Greek views: Thucydides, Socrates, Plato, Aristotle, Stoic, Epicureanism

   b. Religious Traditions

   c. Law and Justice: Epictetus, Aquinas, Hobbes, Locke, Rousseau, Jefferson, Kant, Royce, King, Rawls, Nozick

   d. Consequentialist Ethics: Epicurus, Smith, Bentham, Mill, Rand

   e. Feminist/Womanist Ethics: Gilligan, Nodding

III. Ethical Analysis of Real World Issues – 50%

   a. Morality, relationships, and sexuality (e.g. pornography, adultery, prostitution, LGBT)

   b. Life and death issues (e.g. abortion, euthanasia, suicide, assisted suicide)

   c. Economic issues (inequality, poverty, equal opportunity commodification)

   d. Civil rights (racism, affirmative action)

   e. Punishment (e.g. capital punishment, retributive justice)

   f. War and peace (e.g. just war tradition)

   g. Life centered and human centered ethics (e.g. animals, environmental issues)

   h. Human rights

   i. Biomedical ethics (e.g. experimentation, embryonic stem cell research, human subjects, organ donation)

Chapter 2

Ethics in America Diagnostic Test

DIAGNOSTIC TEST ANSWER SHEET

1. Ⓐ Ⓑ Ⓒ Ⓓ	8. Ⓐ Ⓑ Ⓒ Ⓓ	15. Ⓐ Ⓑ Ⓒ Ⓓ
2. Ⓐ Ⓑ Ⓒ Ⓓ	9. Ⓐ Ⓑ Ⓒ Ⓓ	16. Ⓐ Ⓑ Ⓒ Ⓓ
3. Ⓐ Ⓑ Ⓒ Ⓓ	10. Ⓐ Ⓑ Ⓒ Ⓓ	17. Ⓐ Ⓑ Ⓒ Ⓓ
4. Ⓐ Ⓑ Ⓒ Ⓓ	11. Ⓐ Ⓑ Ⓒ Ⓓ	18. Ⓐ Ⓑ Ⓒ Ⓓ
5. Ⓐ Ⓑ Ⓒ Ⓓ	12. Ⓐ Ⓑ Ⓒ Ⓓ	19. Ⓐ Ⓑ Ⓒ Ⓓ
6. Ⓐ Ⓑ Ⓒ Ⓓ	13. Ⓐ Ⓑ Ⓒ Ⓓ	20. Ⓐ Ⓑ Ⓒ Ⓓ
7. Ⓐ Ⓑ Ⓒ Ⓓ	14. Ⓐ Ⓑ Ⓒ Ⓓ	

ETHICS IN AMERICA DIAGNOSTIC TEST

Directions: Carefully read each of the following 20 questions. Choose the best answer to each question and fill in the corresponding circle on the answer sheet. The Answer Key and Explanations can be found following this Diagnostic Test.

1. Which of the following thinkers developed the philosophy of utilitarianism?

   A. Bentham
   B. Nozick
   C. Smith
   D. Mill

2. For a Stoic, the ethical evaluation of a decision to commit suicide depends on whether it

   A. adheres to basic liberties.
   B. seems to be a reasonable act.
   C. appears to be God's will.
   D. increases overall happiness.

3. The Universal Declaration of Human Rights (UDHR)

   A. was issued after the Rwandan genocide in 1994.
   B. has proven ineffective because it is not legally binding anywhere in the world.
   C. was drafted by the International Criminal Court.
   D. has influenced nations to adopt laws to preserve basic human rights for their citizens.

4. Intentionally withholding treatment in order to allow a patient to die is

   A. active euthanasia.
   B. suicide.
   C. passive euthanasia.
   D. murder.

5. Compatibilists believe that an individual's actions and decisions

    A. are completely governed by uncontrollable natural forces.
    B. cannot influence future events.
    C. are only mental processes.
    D. can involve the exercise of free will.

6. The Hippocratic Oath is a foundational text in what field?

    A. Political science
    B. Biomedical ethics
    C. Feminism
    D. Academia

7. A supporter of affirmative action would argue that

    A. cultural diversity is not important.
    B. ethnicity and income should be factors in college admissions.
    C. the history of racial segregation is no longer relevant.
    D. college applicants should be evaluated solely by standardized test scores.

8. From what text do both Jews and Christians derive moral principles?

    A. Old Testament
    B. New Testament
    C. The Talmud
    D. The Catechism

9. Which of the following philosophies bases morality on the consequences of a behavior?

    A. Determinism
    B. Objectivism
    C. Utilitarianism
    D. Idealism

10. For a subjectivist, the statement "murder is wrong" is

    A. an objective truth.
    B. an expression of personal perception.
    C. supported by scientific evidence.
    D. an objective falsehood.

11. Relativism is the philosophical theory that

A. some moral systems are inherently more valid than others.
B. different people have different standards of behavior.
C. rights are decided by popular consensus.
D. morality involves absolute truths.

12. Which of these is NOT a goal of rehabilitative punishment?

A. Improve quality of life for inmates
B. Reduce overall crime rate
C. Prevent criminals from reentering society
D. Provide inmates with useful skills and education

13. Which of the following is NOT a monotheistic religion?

A. Islam
B. Judaism
C. Hinduism
D. Christianity

14. According to Just War theory, all of the following are important criteria for war EXCEPT:

A. Right intentions
B. Majority in favor
C. Possibility of success
D. Matches provocation

15. Which of the following statements best describes *anthropocentrism*?

A. Humans are the most important living organisms.
B. Men are superior to women.
C. All creatures are equally important.
D. Humans should not control the lives of animals.

16. For a utilitarian, the ethical evaluation of the decision to have an abortion will NOT depend on whether the abortion will

A. cause emotional pain for the woman's family.
B. eliminate pain for the woman having the abortion.
C. cause suffering for the woman having the abortion.
D. instigate change for the woman and her family.

17. The approach that women take when making moral decisions is known as

    A. ethics of feminists.
    B. ethics of justice.
    C. ethics of care.
    D. ethics of empathy.

18. Which Hindu term refers to a person's actions determining what happens to them in the future?

    A. Nirvana
    B. Karma
    C. Dharma
    D. Ahisma

19. Supporters of distributive justice are primarily concerned with what societal issue?

    A. Institutional racism
    B. Economic inequality
    C. Misogyny
    D. Homophobia

20. Aquinas was able to draw a connection between

    A. mathematics and knowledge.
    B. happiness and morality.
    C. theology and science.
    D. faith and virtue.

ANSWER KEY AND EXPLANATIONS

1. A	5. D	9. C	13. C	17. C
2. B	6. B	10. B	14. B	18. B
3. D	7. B	11. B	15. A	19. B
4. C	8. A	12. C	16. D	20. C

1. **The correct answer is A.** Jeremy Bentham first developed the concept of British utilitarianism. Mill (choice D) was a utilitarian inspired by Bentham, but he did not first develop the philosophy. Nozick (choice B) and Smith (choice C) were not utilitarian philosophers.

2. **The correct answer is B.** For a Stoic, the ethical evaluation of a decision to commit suicide depends on whether it seems to be a reasonable act. In cases where a person has a debilitating disease for which there is no treatment, suicide would most likely be considered moral to a Stoic. A utilitarian bases decisions on whether overall happiness increases (choice D). Choices A and C are incorrect.

3. **The correct answer is D.** The Universal Declaration of Human Rights (UDHR) was issued by the United Nations in 1948; thus choices A and C are incorrect. Although it is not legally binding anywhere in the world, some or all of its thirty articles have been adapted by sovereign nations for use in their own laws. It has been used in various international treaties and other human rights-related documents around the world, including the International Bill of Rights, so it is far from being ineffective (choice B).

4. **The correct answer is C.** Passive euthanasia refers to the act of intentionally withholding treatment in order to allow a patient to die. Active euthanasia (choice A) refers to intentionally killing a patient by lethal injection, smothering, or some other method. Suicide (choice B) and murder (choice D) are incorrect.

5. **The correct answer is D.** Compatibilists believe that the theories of determinism and free will are compatible and that an individual's actions and decisions, while influenced by prior causes, also involve the exercise of free will. Hard determinists, on the other hand, believe that actions and decisions are completely governed by uncontrollable natural forces (choice A). Compatibilists believe that an individual can influence future events and that decisions are more than only mental processes, making choices B and C incorrect.

6. **The correct answer is B.** The Hippocratic Oath is a foundational text in biomedical ethics. Composed by the Greek physician Hippocrates in the fifth century BCE, the oath establishes ethical standards that most modern doctors follow, such as maintaining patient confidentiality and not causing intentional injury. Choices A, C, and D are incorrect.

7. **The correct answer is B.** Supporters of affirmative action believe that diversity is important in schools and workplaces and that traditional markers of success, such as high standardized test scores, cannot always be achieved by students and applicants disadvantaged by racism and economic inequality. They therefore enact admissions and hiring policies that give special consideration to factors such as race, ethnicity, and income, alongside other academic and/or career achievements. Therefore, choices A, C, and D are incorrect.

8. **The correct answer is A.** Jews and Christians both derive moral values from the Old Testament, which includes the Five Books of Moses (Genesis, Exodus, Leviticus, Numbers, and Deuteronomy). The New Testament (choice B) is a source of ethical teachings for Christians only, while the Talmud (choice C) is a series of Jewish legal books. The Catechism (choice D) is a core text of the Catholic Church and is not read by Jews.

9. **The correct answer is C.** Utilitarianism, which is also known as consequentialism, is the philosophy that actions are morally acceptable if good consequences outweigh bad consequences. On the other hand, an action is considered immoral if bad consequences outweigh good consequences. Determinism asserts that events occur because of natural laws, so choice A is incorrect. Choices B and D are not based on consequences.

10. **The correct answer is B.** Subjectivism is the philosophical theory that there is no absolute truth, but rather, all statements are reducible to personal preferences and perceptions. Empiricism is the philosophical theory that absolute truths can be determined through scientific experimentation and evidence (choice C). Choices A and D are incorrect.

11. **The correct answer is B.** Moral relativism is the philosophical theory that different people have different standards of behavior. A relativist might argue, for example, that cannibalism is no less moral than eating a vegetarian diet. The theory that rights are determined by popular consensus (choice C) is typically associated with Immanuel Kant's notion of the "common good." Choices A and D are incorrect.

12. **The correct answer is C.** Rehabilitation provides convicted criminals an education and other opportunities for personal growth while they are imprisoned. The objective of a rehabilitative prison system is to make life inside prison more productive and harmonious and to prepare prisoners for their eventual release. Because educated and skilled individuals are considered less likely to commit further crimes, rehabilitated prisoners are allowed to reenter society. Therefore, choices A, B, and D are incorrect.

13. **The correct answer is C.** There are many Hindu gods according to followers of Hinduism. Islam, Judaism, and Christianity are monotheisms, meaning that followers believe in the existence of one God and no other higher beings. Thus, choices A, B, and D are incorrect.

14. **The correct answer is B.** According to Just War theory, a war is justified if it is fought with the right intentions (choice A), if there is a reasonable chance for success (choice C), and if the actions match the provocation (choice D). The opinion of the majority (choice B) is not a criterium.

15. **The correct answer is A.** Anthropocentrism is the philosophical theory that humans are inherently superior to other living organisms, and thus, humans have the right to exert control over natural processes. Choice B describes *androcentrism*—a male-focused philosophical perspective—rather than anthropocentrism. Choices C and D are incorrect.

16. **The correct answer is D.** A utilitarian views ethical decisions in terms of good and bad consequences. If the overall consequences are bad, then a decision is immoral. Choices A, B, and C affect the overall happiness or unhappiness of the people involved, so these are factors in the decision. Choice D is irrelevant, which means it is the correct answer.

17. **The correct answer is C.** The concept of ethics of care was developed by psychologist Carol Gilligan, who asserts that women consider responsibilities and relationships when making decisions. The moral decisions made by women often appeal to such emotions as sympathy, love, and concern. The ethics of justice (choice B) is what Gilligan believes is the male approach to decision making, based on application of rules and minimizing emotions. Choices A and D are incorrect.

18. **The correct answer is B.** Karma is the Hindu and Buddhist principle that a person's actions determine what happens to them in the future and in future reincarnations. Nirvana refers to a state of bliss, so choice A is incorrect. Dharma (choice C) refers to the duties that must be fulfilled based on a person's caste. Ahisma (choice D) is the way a person acts or feels about others.

19. **The correct answer is B.** Proponents of distributive justice are concerned with economic inequality. They argue that wide disparities in income are detrimental to the common good and that with redistribution of money, goods, and services—such as welfare, educational scholarships, and health care— society can be more just and harmonious. Choices A, C, and D are incorrect.

20. **The correct answer is C.** St. Thomas Aquinas was a thir-teenth-century Catholic priest who drew a connection between theology and science. Aquinas believed that learning about nature was a way to learn about God. Choices A, B, and D are incorrect.

DIAGNOSTIC TEST ASSESSMENT GRID

Now that you've completed the diagnostic test and read through the answer explanations, you can use your results to target your studying. Find the question numbers from the diagnostic test that you answered incorrectly and highlight or circle them below. Then focus extra attention on the sections dealing with those topics.

Ethics in America

Content Area	Topic	Question #
Ethical Traditions	• Greek views • Religious traditions • Law and justice • Consequentialist ethics • Feminist/Womanist ethics	1, 2, 9, 13, 17 18, 20
Contemporary Foundational Issues	• Relativism • Subjectivism • Determinism and free will • Relationship between morality and religion	5, 8, 10,11
Ethical Analysis of Issues and Practical Applications	• Morality, relationships, and sexuality • Life and death issues • Economic issues • Civil Rights • Punishment • War and peace • Life-centered and human-centered ethics • Human rights • Biomedical ethics	3, 4, 6, 7, 12, 14, 15, 16, 19

Chapter 3

Ethics in America Subject Review

ETHICAL TRADITIONS

Ethics refers to the academic discipline of analyzing morality. Reasoning, rules, and logic form the basis of ethical philosophy. The foundation of American ethics began thousands of years ago in Ancient Greece when philosophers such as Socrates, Plato, and Aristotle first began discussing virtue, justice, and politics.

Greek Views

Since at least 1200 BCE, myths and stories provided explanations for virtually everything in Greek life from floods to war battles. Greek gods and goddesses resembled human beings, and mythology focused on the activities of Earth's residents. The Greek worldview considered people the center of everything, and the world was a playground for traveling, building societies, and engaging in warfare. Change occurred in the sixth century BCE when pre-Socratic philosophers raised questions about the natural world. How was the world made? How does the world work? The theories of cosmology and cosmogony developed at this time. **Cosmology** is the study of the physical world, such as what it is made of and how it works. **Cosmogony** is the study of the origin of the universe, such as how it came into existence.

One of the most notable pre-Socratic philosophers was Pythagoras, who was also a mathematician and a cosmologist. Since Pythagoras wrote nothing, his exact philosophy is uncertain. However, evidence suggests that beliefs in the magic of numbers and reincarnation were aspects of his philosophy. The philosopher had a significant number of followers, perhaps because people believed he had miraculous powers.

TIP: Most of the criticism aimed against the Sophists regarded their reliance on persuasion and manipulation, rather than the truth.

The Sophists

The first philosophers in Greece studied nature, but philosophical focus shifted to man toward the second half of the fifth century BCE. The democratic system in Athens was evolving, and it was the duty of every free adult male to participate in government. Because of the interest in society and politics among Athens citizens, a group of teachers known as the Sophists emerged. The Sophists traveled throughout Greece giving lectures about various popular topics, such as rhetoric, history, mathematics, and politics. Sophists received large sums of money in exchange for their presentations, unlike the wise men of Greece who freely shared their thoughts with the public.

The public viewed the first Sophists as teachers of virtue and excellence rather than as philosophers. Protagoras, one of the earliest and most respected Sophists, is best known for stating, "Man is the measure of all things." The statement suggests that people rather than nature determine behavior. Many experts consider the Sophists the first relativists. Ethical relativism proposes that every point of view is equally valid and that different people have different standards of behavior. Relativists often rely more heavily on persuasion than on truth. In addition, Protagoras questioned the existence of gods and thought that individuals should act according to their best interests without searching for wisdom from a higher power.

While many early Sophists were admired, others drew criticism for being untrustworthy. Some Sophists made boastful assertions that they could prove any position without knowledge of the subject matter. The term *sophistry*, which means to use purposely deceptive and invalid arguments, derives its meaning from actions of the Sophists. Despite the fact that the Sophists emphasized persuasive skills rather than the honest analysis of issues, they set the stage for intellectual discussion in Athens.

Thucydides

In 431 BCE, war broke out between Athens and Sparta. Thucydides, a Greek historian, wrote *The History of the Peloponnesian War* as a report of the battle that lasted until 404 BCE. *The History of the Peloponnesian War* provides a graphic and exact account of military actions. Thucydides objectively presented the factual events of the war without any attribution to mythological beings. Yet he added drama to the document with the inclusion of fictional speeches that are factual in content. Considered one of the first and greatest historians, Thucydides raised questions in his publication about the ethics of war, especially with regard to justice and power.

Socrates

Socrates, one of the most influential thinkers of all times, lived in Athens during the fifth century BCE. Socrates was an outspoken critic of the Sophists, Athenian politics, and religious institutions. Socrates considered the teachings of the Sophists empty and manipulative, and he debated with them frequently. Socrates sought to uncover truth and spent much of his time discussing virtue, justice, and morality with the citizens of Athens. During the time of Socrates, most people equated virtue with beauty, and the philosopher hoped to change that notion. Socrates hoped to elevate the moral and intellectual nature of the city, and he sacrificed everything he had in this attempt.

Most information about Socrates' teachings stems from the writings of his most famous student, Plato, because Socrates never wrote any books. Socrates is renowned more for the way in which he taught than a specific philosophy. Socrates employed a questioning technique, later termed the Socratic Method or dialectic, to discuss philosophical issues with people. The method involves asking a series of questions and drawing out answers from students to develop understanding and insight about a particular issue. Socrates' series of questions eventually weakened the other person's argument by pointing out contradictions. Most of the time, Socrates claimed that he lacked any knowledge of the subject to illustrate that answers existed in the mind of the student.

Plato

Socrates' most famous student, Plato, was a philosopher and mathematician. After the death of Socrates, Plato continued with his teacher's work and established **the Academy** in 387 BCE. The Academy, which is considered the first university, served as the most significant institution of higher learning in the Western world. There, teachers and students discussed and researched mathematics, astronomy, politics, and natural history. Plato's earliest writings, the Socratic dialogues, convey the ideas of his deceased teacher. A dialogue is a method of presenting ideas in the format of a fictional discussion with other people, which for Plato was usually Socrates.

Plato's most famous and influential work is *The Republic*. The text uses dialogues to examine whether it is always better to be just than unjust. Unhappy with the democracy and tyranny of Greek government, Plato believed that selfish individuals wielded too much power. Plato's discussion of an ideal republic, known as utopian thinking, led to his conclusion that the ideal state is divided into three classes of citizens. The guardians of society are philosopher-kings. Philosopher-kings are capable of understanding truth and justice and are guided by wisdom rather than self-interest. Soldiers serve as the next level of Plato's ideal society because they are unselfish, moral, and courageous. The final societal level consists of workers or producers who are motivated by a certain level of greed, which Plato refers to as appetite. In Plato's ideal state, political justice replaces democracy and tyranny.

In *The Republic*, Plato employed an extended metaphor known as the Allegory of the Cave to compare untutored people to prisoners in a cave. The prisoners misinterpret shadows on a wall as reality. The parable and the rest of *The Republic* illustrate Plato's primary philosophical convictions:

- The world experienced through the senses is not the real world, which can only be understood intellectually.
- Some people are less virtuous than others, which is why government is necessary.
- Enlightened people have a responsibility to society.

As with other Greeks of the fourth and fifth century BCE, Plato believed in pursuing personal excellence to achieve peace in a troubled world. Plato explains in *The Republic* that the world may not acknowledge or reward virtue, but ultimate happiness can only be achieved through virtue.

Aristotle

One of the most renowned students of Plato's Academy in Athens was the philosopher Aristotle. In addition to being a philosopher, Aristotle was an authority on nearly every subject, including ethics, physics, biology, and psychology. However, Aristotle's approach to philosophy differed significantly from his teacher's methods. Whereas Plato viewed the world in abstracts, Aristotle concentrated on observations and experiences, or empirical knowledge. Learning about so many subjects corresponds with two key beliefs of Aristotle:

1. Everything has a purpose.
2. Change is both necessary and natural.

According to Aristotle, living virtuously is the purpose of human beings in the world. In his book *Nicomachean Ethics*, Aristotle states that physical pleasures derived from money, work, and sex fail to bring ultimate happiness. Aristotle equates virtue to happiness, and he distinguishes between two types of virtues—moral excellence and intellectual excellence. Moral virtues, which indicate excellence of character, include self-control, bravery, self-respect, gentleness, truthfulness, and generosity. Intellectual virtues include scientific knowledge, intuitive reason, practical wisdom, and skill. From Aristotle's perspective, maintaining balance and not going to the extreme in either direction is the key to happiness. This concept is known as the **golden mean**.

Stoics and Hedonists

From the fourth through the first centuries BCE, the philosophy of Plato and Aristotle spread to other countries along the Mediterranean Sea. During this period, multiple groups of thought emerged, including the Stoics and the Hedonists.

Founded around 300 BCE by a philosopher named Zeno, **Stoicism** later influenced Christian thinkers and experienced a revival during the Renaissance. Stoicism is a philosophy based on the idea that absolute law rules the universe and that humans cannot change fate. According to Stoic ethics, virtue requires living and acting according to reason and self-control. Wise and happy people are content with whatever occurs in life because they realize everything is inevitable. Unhappiness occurs when a person feels disappointment or regret about a certain course of events. Epictetus, one of the most prominent Stoics of the second century AD, encouraged his students to "live according to nature." Epictetus, a Roman slave often tortured by his master, exemplified the Stoic philosophy by refusing to moan during beatings because he accepted his fate in life.

Also around 300 BCE, the philosophy of **Hedonism**, or **Epicureanism**, emerged under the guidance of Epicurus. The philosopher asserted that happiness was the purpose of life. According to hedonism, achieving happiness involves avoiding pain and increasing pleasure. Epicurus asserted that the universe was created by an accidental collision of atoms rather than by Greek gods. While Epicurus did not deny the existence of gods and goddesses, he suggested that they are indifferent to the activities of humans. Upon death, people's souls and bodies would dissolve back into atoms. As a result, hedonists felt free to enjoy life to the greatest extent without worrying about retribution from the gods.

RELIGIOUS TRADITIONS

The Bible has been the most popular tool for teaching morality in the Western world and serves as the center point for Judeo-Christian ethics. The Bible was first translated into Greek around 250 BCE, and it offered a completely different approach to ethics than the Greek philosophers did. For the Israelites, morality resided in one righteous God, and God's teachings were the basis of their laws.

Jews and Christians share the moral principles found in the Hebrew Bible, or Old Testament. The Ten Commandments are a list of rules indicating that it is immoral to murder, commit adultery, steal, and covet. Stories throughout the Old Testament indicate the importance of obeying God, taking responsibility, and exhibiting willpower. Whereas Judaism is based only on the Old Testament, Christianity also includes the teachings of Jesus Christ, found in the New Testament. The New Testament provides numerous ethical principles, most of which are focused on the concept of love. Christians are instructed to love God above all else and to love their neighbors, as indicated by the story of the Good Samaritan.

Although the Bible has been the most significant source of morality in America since the first colonists arrived, other religious traditions have had an effect on Western society as well. The following table provides a general overview of the major world religions.

Major World Religions	
Christianity	Bible instructs that personal salvation occurs through faith and that God is merciful and all knowing.
Judaism	As the oldest monotheistic religion, Judaism places importance on history, laws, and religious community and is responsible for influencing both Islam and Christianity.
Islam	Koran believed to have been written by the prophet Mohammed under the direction of God. Muslims are instructed to be generous and obedient and to avoid being greedy or prideful.

| Hinduism | Moral guidance based on a principle called ahimsa, which is the principle of nonviolence. Ahisma involves both behavior and feelings towards others, so hatred for another violates ahisma. Emphasis is on being detached from pain and desire and choosing actions that cause the least amount of harm. |
| Buddhism | Moral code does not have a divine origin. Dalai Lama asserts that morality helps people achieve happiness many times through reincarnation. Happiness to self and others derives from being loving, compassionate, patient, forgiving, and responsible. |

The concepts of **karma** and **dharma** are connected with both Hinduism and Buddhism. Karma is the principle that a person's actions determine what happens to them in the future and in future reincarnations. Dharma refers to the righteous duties of a person toward people and gods. In contrast, the three monotheistic religions—Judaism, Christianity, and Islam—consider events in life as being the will of God. **Monotheism** means belief in only one god rather than multiple gods.

Many countries around the world have a national religion. In some, religious concepts of morality and justice heavily influence the law of the land. In the United States, numerous laws reflect the Judeo-Christian morality of some of the nation's founders, as well as the moral perspectives of a majority of the current population. Laws prohibiting murder, theft, and slavery, for example, can be traced back to Biblical precepts. Yet there is also a commonly accepted "separation of church and state." Though that phrase does not technically appear in the Constitution, the First Amendment does state: "Congress shall make no law respecting an establishment of religion, or prohibiting the free exercise thereof." Most legal scholars interpret this statute as saying that while everyone is free to practice (or not practice) religion, religious morals and rules do not override secular law. The First Amendment also protects religious institutions from government intrusion.

LAW AND JUSTICE

Natural law theories are based on the idea that the moral standards guiding human behavior originate in human nature and the universe. Deviating from the norm is immoral, sinful, evil, and harmful. However, the disorder caused by deviation forces a reasoning individual to restore events back to normal. Such logic is based on the idea that the universe is morally neutral and that moral laws are part of nature. The attraction of natural law is its ability to provide meaning for life and behavior. Elements of natural law are evident in the beliefs of the Ancient Greeks and the Stoics.

TIP: Aquinas viewed nature as a way to understand and draw close to God.

Aquinas's Natural Law Theory

Many medieval philosophers adopted natural law theories in an attempt to explain the relationship between God and humanity. Thirteenth-century Catholic priest St. Thomas Aquinas believed that faith and reason could exist together, and that theology and science were not contradictory. Well versed in the philosophy of Aristotle, Aquinas wrote that learning about nature is a way to learn about God. Aquinas's **theory of natural law** asserts that the laws discovered in nature stem from the eternal God. Human beings are naturally rational, so it is moral for humans to behave rationally.

Political Theories

In addition to questions about nature, numerous philosophers have raised questions about political authorities and the best way to manage societies. **Social contract theory** refers to the idea that the right to rule and the obligation to obey are based upon an agreement between an individual and society. The moral code put forth in a social contract creates a harmonious society in which all parties work together for mutual advantage. Thomas Hobbes, John Locke, and Jean-Jacques Rousseau wrote about social contract theory during the seventeenth and eighteenth centuries. As the most well-known social contract theorists, they attempted to explain how people join society for the purpose of security and societal order.

Thomas Hobbes

Thomas Hobbes, a seventeenth-century English political philosopher, developed a theory suggesting that humans live fearfully in a natural world full of insecurity and violence. *Leviathan*, which Hobbes wrote during the English Civil War, describes the relationship between civil law and natural law. According to Hobbes, fear and insecurity force people into surrendering their natural rights to a sovereign ruler and forming a social contract. Failure to submit to a ruler, even a bad one, will result in conflict and savagery. Hobbes viewed virtues such as gratitude and modesty as traits that help people live harmoniously with the rest of society. He believed that it is in the self-interest of individuals to have such characteristics.

John Locke

Seventeenth-century British philosopher John Locke provided his thoughts about government in numerous writings, and he is often associated with the concept of empiricism. **Empiricism** refers to the notion that reliable knowledge is acquired by testing ideas against sensory evidence. Locke proposed that humans are not born with any ideas because the mind is a blank slate at birth. Understanding develops as people see, hear, and touch things.

Locke spent much of his efforts questioning the structure of British government. For centuries, people held that kings were direct descendants of Adam and thus had the divine right to rule. However, the bloodshed resulting from recent wars caused Locke to raise concerns about the monarchy. In *Two Treatises of Government*, Locke explains the function of political authority and proposes that individuals have certain natural rights:

- The right to live without being harmed by others
- The right to make their own choices
- The right to own property

According to Locke, the purpose of political authority is to protect individual rights to life, liberty, and property. Underlying Locke's theory is the idea that people have the right to resist unjust political authority. When a political power fails to uphold its half of a social contract, citizens should resist and revolt to protect their rights.

Locke's revolutionary ideas about government influenced many others, including Thomas Jefferson and the Founding Fathers in writing the U.S. Declaration of Independence: *We hold these truths to be self-evident, that all men are created equal, that they are endowed by their Creator with certain unalienable rights, that among these are life, liberty, and the pursuit of happiness.*

Jean-Jacques Rousseau

Locke also influenced Jean-Jacques Rousseau, the eighteenth-century French philosopher. Rousseau believed that human beings are innately good but that society, with its desires and greed, corrupts them. Rousseau developed the concept of **general will** in *Discourse on Political Economy* and *The Social Contract*. Under general will, citizens act as legislators to determine, as a collective body, the laws and legislation of society. According to the concept of general will, power rests with the citizens, and society becomes highly democratic. The French government banned Rousseau's controversial writings, and the philosopher fled to Switzerland.

John Rawls and Robert Nozick

Two American philosophers of the twentieth century are known for their ideas regarding political philosophy. John Rawls, author of *A Theory of Justice*, revived the social contract theory. Most of Rawls's writings raised questions about **distributive justice**, which refers to the way in which benefits and burdens are allocated within a society. Rawls attempted to refute the philosophy of utilitarianism based on the concept of "justice as fairness":

- **First principle:** Each person is to have an equal right to the most extensive total system of equal basic liberties compatible with a similar system of liberty for all.
- **Second principle:** Social and economic inequalities are to be arranged so that they are both: A. to the greatest benefit of the least advantaged, and B. attached to offices and positions open to all under conditions of fair equality of opportunity.

According to Rawls, the first principle has priority over the second principle, which is known as the difference principle. So, basic liberties, like freedom of speech, should not be hindered to improve life for the least advantaged individuals in a society. Rawls summed up his philosophy when he stated, "Injustice is simply inequalities that are not to the benefit of all."

One of Rawls's colleagues at Harvard, Robert Nozick, also addressed the concept of distributive justice. However, Nozick compared income tax to forced labor and stated that the redistribution of wealth is only justifiable when it is resolving a past injustice.

Immanuel Kant

Eighteenth-century German philosopher Immanuel Kant is one of the greatest influences on Western philosophy. Much of Kant's work attempts to answer three primary questions:

1. What can I know?
2. What should I do?
3. What can I hope for?

The concept of **transcendental idealism** plays a significant role in Kant's philosophy, as well as the philosophy of other German idealists. *Transcendence* means to be beyond the experience. Transcendental idealism is the concept that appearances should be viewed as only representations and not as things themselves. In other words, both the mind and understanding create reality. Kant used four categories of understanding—space, time, causality, and substance—to explain how the mind structures reality and enables people to make sense of experiences. Kant referred to these four concepts as *a priori* concepts to explain that the concepts occurred before a person's existence.

In addition, Kant developed two categories of moral thought: **practical reason** and **pure reason**. Practical reason is reasoning about how people should act, and pure reason is reasoning about what actually exists. **Categorical imperatives** are universal moral laws that act as the basis of practical reason and that help people behave morally. According to Kant, a behavior conforms to a categorical imperative if it is moral for all human beings.

CONSEQUENTIALIST ETHICS

Moral Egoism

Best known as the author of *The Wealth of Nations*, Adam Smith was more than a founder of **capitalism**. He was also an eighteenth-century moral philosopher. Smith proposed that the common good of society advances when individuals focus on benefiting themselves, a concept related to moral egoism. The theory of moral egoism asserts that it is always moral to act in a manner that benefits self-interest. According to Smith, individuals are able to achieve happiness in life when they focus on their own happiness rather than the happiness of others.

Ayn Rand, a twentieth-century Russian philosopher, also falls into the category of **moral egoist**. Rand asserted that pursuing self-interests and personal happiness are "the highest moral purpose" of life. According to Rand's philosophy of objectivism, doing anything for another person will sacrifice happiness unless there is a material or psychological reward involved. Rand's writings indicate her objection to the weak exploiting the strong and her admiration for individual accomplishment.

Utilitarianism

Utilitarianism, or **consequentialism**, refers to the theory that actions are morally acceptable if good consequences outweigh bad consequences. Similarly, if bad consequences outweigh good consequences, an action is morally wrong. Therefore, morality is completely about the results of any behavior. A utilitarian does not seek answers to ethical dilemmas from the universe, but from within. Behavior that brings pleasure is moral, while behavior that brings pain is immoral.

Jeremy Bentham (1748–1832) modified the philosophy of Epicurus, the first utilitarian, by arguing that service to society generates more pleasure than service to self. As the founder of British utilitarianism, Bentham asserted that behavior is wrong if it reduces overall happiness. For Bentham, behavior that produces long-term happiness to the community is preferred to short-term personal happiness. Bentham defines happiness as experiencing pleasure and avoiding pain. Bentham's ideas motivated the Philosophical Radicals, a group of social reformers in the early part of the nineteenth century. The Radicals advocated universal male suffrage and politics geared toward human happiness instead of natural rights.

Bentham's work inspired nineteenth-century British philosopher John Stuart Mill, whose father was a member of the Radicals. Mill conveyed his utilitarian ideas in numerous pieces, but his essay *On Liberty* is the best-known. In the essay, Mill asserts that the only time a government has the moral authority to limit a person's liberty is when harm may occur otherwise. In all other situations, people should be allowed the freedom to behave as desired. Continuing with utilitarian concepts, Mill wrote *The Subjugation of Women* as an argument in favor of women's equality. Mill asserts that the marital relationship improves when both partners have equal roles.

FEMINIST/WOMANIST ETHICS

Feminism refers to the philosophical and political discourse geared toward exposing, analyzing, and addressing sexual inequality. Feminist philosophy emerged in the 1960s for a number of reasons. First, it was believed that the bulk of philosophical research omitted women from major studies. Second, it was believed that there was a masculine bias in philosophical research, so an accurate assessment of women's morals was either neglected or distorted.

Carol Gilligan is a psychologist best known for her research and writings about the moral development of women. Unlike feminists who assert that there are no differences between men and women, Gilligan indicates that women and men have different approaches to making moral decisions. Men, she believes, follow the ethics of justice and focus on applying rules and minimizing emotions when making decisions. For example, Kant's categorical imperatives and utilitarianism are both masculine approaches to making decisions. In contrast, she contends that women tend more to the ethics of care and consider responsibilities and relationships when making decisions. The moral decisions made by women often appeal to such emotions as sympathy, love, and concern. Gilligan argues that both types of ethics are valuable to society.

Philosopher Nel Noddings also studies the concept of ethics of care. Noddings has focused her research on the origins of care within the home, such as parent-child relationships. Noddings asserts that studying how people care for those around them leads to understanding how to care for people within society.

CONTEMPORARY FOUNDATIONAL ISSUES

Determinism and Free Will

Do we as human beings have the ability to make spontaneous choices and exercise free will? Or is every action and decision predetermined by unchangeable natural processes? Can we know that we are free, and does it matter—morally or legally—whether we are or aren't? These are the questions at the heart of the theory of **determinism**.

Determinists assert that everything results from a cause, whether known or hidden, and that prior events directly influence future events. Determinism is not as rigid as the theory of fatalism, which argues that the origins of the universe set in motion an absolutely inescapable course of history and that all events proceed according to one certain destiny. Nevertheless, determinists do assert that certain causes necessarily produce certain effects. These causes can range from the physical laws of the universe, such as the movement of electrons within an atom, to social and environmental factors, such as education and childhood experiences. The eighteenth-century philosopher Baron d'Holbach theorized that, because the chemical matter in the human brain is subject to the laws of physics and biology, all human thought and perception is determined by those laws as well. Thus all actions, from taking a single step to committing a violent crime, should be seen as a consequence of chemical reactions rather than the outcome of independent moral choice.

More recently, the psychologist B.F. Skinner proposed that free will was an illusion and that external stimuli such as positive reinforcement, negative reinforcement, and punishment determine our patterns of behavior. He demonstrated, through laboratory experiments on rats, that introducing or withholding certain stimuli to a situation greatly increased the probability of certain behaviors and actions. He called this practice "operant condi- tioning." As with d'Holbach's theory, Skinner's experiments raised signif- icant questions about whether an individual can be held morally or legally responsible for his or her actions, if inputs such as punishment or reward make certain future actions inevitable.

Compatibilists, by contrast, argue that while the laws of nature do influ- ence our behavior, we can also make choices that subvert established patterns and prevent supposed inevitabilities. Put simply, compatibilists believe free will is not an illusion. Some ethicists take this position on theo- logical grounds, such as the early Christian philosopher Augustine, who argued that God granted humans the freedom to act or not act based on our impulses. Others take a more secular approach, pointing at scientific evidence that shows that despite the laws of physics, random and unpre- dictable events can and do occur. The question of moral responsibility is thus arguably less complicated for compatibilists; if free will does exist, then individuals who commit moral and legal offenses do so knowingly and by their own volition. Members of society may then exercise their own volition to punish (or not punish) the offender accordingly.

Relativism and Subjectivism

Humans abide by (and likewise reject) countless moral and ethical systems, many of which we have explored: stoicism, hedonism, utilitarianism, moral egoism, idealism, feminism, etc. Many of these systems, such as hedonism and moral egoism, are compatible and have overlapping principles and val- ues. Others, particularly religious belief systems, have less in common, and their differences have historically created tension and conflict.

Which one of these ethical systems is inherently better than all the others? Which one should you personally follow? Which will produce the most happiness—that is, if being happy is the purpose of life after all? Two phil- osophical theories, relativism and subjectivism, do not provide precise instruction for living a meaningful life or compel followers to adhere to certain norms. Rather, they are "metaethical" theories. They analyze the relationships *between* ethical systems; explore the value and effect of ethical statements and judgments; and consider whether any absolute ethical truth is ever possible.

Relativism is the theory that there is no such thing as an unconditional or universal ethical truth. Rather, all ethical practices are circumstantial— they reflect social, cultural, or personal situations. Different practices and ethics may be right for different people at different places and times. When traveling to another country, for example, it is typical to set aside the customs practiced at home and adopt the hosts' customs, reflecting a belief that there is inherent value to ways of life other than one's own. Relativists also make the point that social mores and scientific ideas have changed greatly over several millennia, and that we should thus be wary of anyone expressing supposedly absolute claims or infallible truths. Enforcing rigid moral rules and shutting out alternatives can prevent cultural growth and progress.

Subjectivism is the related theory that that there is no such thing as an unconditional or universal ethical truth, specifically because all statements reflect *only* the personal perception of the person saying them. Thus if you said "Rainy days are the worst," you wouldn't be objectively "right," and someone else who loved playing in the rain wouldn't be objectively "wrong"—the two of you would simply have different, yet equally valid perceptions. At first glance, subjectivism would appear to make it impossible for members of society to act and think collectively, since we all exist in our own moral bubbles. In practice, however, many people can and do act on the same common-sense beliefs and instincts, and where there is disagreement, subjectivism suggests compromise and tolerance of others' attitudes. In the subjectivist perspective, ethical statements can gain in value and become actionable when people listening to the statement agree: If millions agree that "murder is a crime," for example, they can build a society and pass laws that reflect that preference, even while recognizing that it's not an absolute truth or fact.

Relationship between Morality and Religion

To discuss the relationship between morality and religion, one must first determine if there is a link between religious views and morals. Many religions provide a framework for values designed to guide members regarding personal behavior and in determining between right and wrong through sources such as holy books, oral and written traditions, and religious leaders. Within the wide range of ethical traditions, religious traditions often share tenets with secular ethical theories such as consequentialism and utilitarianism.

Although the two concepts can be considered as closely related, many ethicists believe religion and morality are not synonymous and that, both in principle and theory, morality and a religious value system are two distinct guides for behavior. Religious values vary greatly, which can affect one's interpretation of what is considered moral. Modern monotheistic religions, such as Christianity, Islam, and Judaism, define right and wrong by the laws and rules set forth by their respective gods and as interpreted by religious leaders within the respective faith. Polytheistic religious traditions, however, tend to be less definitive. For example, in the Buddhist faith, an individual's intention and the circumstances involved in a given situation both play roles in determining whether an action is right or wrong.

For many religious people, morality and religion are the same or inseparable; for them, either morality is a result of practicing their religion or their religion is their morality. For others, especially those who do not adhere to any religion, morality and religion are distinct and separate; religion may be immoral or completely unrelated to morality, and morality may or should have no connection to religion. Debate continues as to whether a moral life can be lived without an absolute lawgiver (a deity) as a guide, and if moral behavior is dependent upon religious beliefs. This controversy is further fueled when questions of ethics arise regarding religions with beliefs that conflict with current social standards.

ETHICAL ANALYSIS OF REAL WORLD ISSUES

The previous section of this review focused on the ethical concepts developed by different philosophers in world history. This section provides a brief overview of some of the ethical issues facing American citizens today.

Morality, Relationships, and Sexuality

Morality regarding sexuality often centers on the idea of sex without marriage, and most of the attention garnered by this topic relates to teens having premarital sex. Many people consider sex outside of marriage morally wrong because God forbids it. However, there are also non-theological perspectives regarding morality and sexuality. According to utilitarianism, if the overall happiness of an unmarried couple increases by having sex, then it is morally acceptable. Yet, possible problems include guilt, sexually transmitted diseases, and unintentional pregnancy, which would all tip the happiness scale in the opposite direction. Both Aristotle and the Dalai Lama focus on long-term rather than temporary happiness, which might not be achieved through a sexual relationship outside of marriage.

Another related issue involves the morality of homosexuality, which raises strong opinions on both sides. While some people believe homosexuality disobeys the will of God or condemn homosexuality because they consider it unnatural, many others argue that sexual orientation—like skin color or left- or right-handedness—is biologically determined and thus should not be subject to discrimination. The argument of natural versus unnatural raises questions about the definition of *natural*. If the meaning of *natural* is *normal*, then some might argue that abnormality does not equal immorality. For example, it is abnormal to jump four feet off the ground, but it is not immoral. Others argue that procreation is the purpose of sexual organs, and homosexual acts are an unnatural use of the body. Based on such a theory, is it immoral to use a foot for propping open a door? Some of the philosophers discussed in the previous section may not have written their views about sexuality, but an understanding of the different theories should provide the basis of an educated guess.

Issues regarding sexuality are often debated within the American legal system. In two Supreme Court cases in the twenty-first century, for example, the court determined that some state laws unfairly discriminated against gay men and women and limited their civil rights. In *Lawrence v. Texas* (2003), the court ruled that laws prohibiting same-sex sexual activity violated the constitutional right to privacy, and in *Obergefell v. Hodges* (2015), the court ruled that laws prohibiting same-sex marriage violated the constitutional right to equal protection under the law.

Opponents frequently contend that while legal protections of homosexuality might benefit some groups and individuals, they might also violate others' rights. For example, the right to religious freedom, protected by the First Amendment, could be threatened if the religiously-based refusal to serve gay customers is a crime punishable by law. The religious perspective on this matter is not monolithic, however. There is an ongoing debate within religious communities about tolerance of LGBT (lesbian, gay, bisexual, and transgender) people: some leaders and adherents argue that texts such as the Bible and Koran compel people to "love their neighbor," while others argue that those texts explicitly prohibit non-heterosexual activity and that laws should reflect that.

Life and Death Issues

Abortion

Abortion has long been a controversial issue in America, especially since the 1973 U.S. Supreme Court handed down its decision in *Roe v. Wade*. In that case, the justices determined that states could not prevent a woman from having an abortion during the first trimester of pregnancy, but could enact regulations related to maternal health in the second trimester and prohibit abortion in the third trimester with exceptions for extraordinary circumstances where it would preserve the life or health of the mother. The justices in the majority based their decision on the right to privacy guaranteed by the U.S. Constitution. The decision in *Roe* has never been reversed entirely, but numerous states have since enacted regulations on abortions in the second and third trimesters of pregnancy.

In the decades since *Roe* was decided, the ethics and politics of abortion have remained heavily debated in the United States. Right-to-life advocates assert that abortion is immoral because the fetus is a living human being from the moment of conception. In contrast, the most liberal view of abortion holds that a woman always has the right to decide what happens to her body at any point during a pregnancy. While these two opinions may represent extremes of the spectrum, many people grapple with whether and when abortion is moral. The following questions are often raised in the abortion debate:

- At what stage of fetal development is abortion acceptable?
- What is the point of viability (when a fetus can live outside of the womb)?
- What are the reasons for seeking an abortion? Rape? Teen pregnancy? Career?

Recent advancements with infertility treatment also raise ethical questions about human life. For many women who are trying to conceive, such treatments are the best or only option to do so. During the process, a medical professional extracts several eggs from a prospective mother's ovaries and artificially inseminates the eggs with sperm from her husband, partner, friend, or an anonymous donor. Later, tests show which eggs have become viable embryos. In a case in which several embryos are viable, should the mother be responsible for carrying them all to term? Some ethicists argue that destroying a viable embryo is morally justifiable, as it is not yet recognizably human, but rather a cluster of cells incapable of thought or feeling. Others argue that all embryos contain potential human life that must be protected, and thus all viable embryos should be implanted or donated intact.

In addition, parents in some cultures desire male babies instead of female babies, so they abort girls. The public funding of abortions raises another concern. Opponents assert that the government should not fund an immoral activity, while advocates claim that a legal abortion should be available to everyone and not just the wealthy.

Suicide

Debate has raged for thousands of years about the morality or immorality of suicide. According to Plato, suicide is wrong unless the gods encourage it. In later writings, Plato indicates disapproval for suicide that occurs from "unmanly cowardice," but he seems to suggest that suicide is acceptable if a person faces hardship, disgrace, or extreme stress. Aristotle apparently agrees that suicide to "fly from evil" is acceptable, but suicide used to "escape from poverty or love" is not. Stoics believe suicide is acceptable when it seems like a reasonable and justifiable act, such as not having to live with a debilitating disease or avoiding being tortured into revealing information to a state enemy. Moreover, many Jews and Christians believe that God prohibits suicide based on the Commandment stating, "You shall not murder."

As indicated by both Plato and Aristotle, the reason for committing suicide often determines whether people view the act as moral or immoral. For example, if a person's quality of life has significantly diminished due to a terminal illness or a crippling disease, then suicide may be a reasonable alternative to living. In other cases, suicide is considered honorable, such as when Buddhist monks burned themselves to death in protest of the Vietnam War. A utilitarian would find suicide moral only if it increased the total happiness of everyone involved. However, Kant thought that suicide was always an immoral act.

Euthanasia

Euthanasia refers to killing or allowing the death of a sick or injured person for the sake of mercy. The act may involve killing someone, perhaps by giving a high dosage of drugs, or letting someone die without attempting to save them. While euthanasia is typically associated with the elderly, the issue relates to all stages of life:

- What should parents do when their infants are born with severe physical defects like an incomplete brain? Should they allow the child to die naturally or allow physicians to inject a lethal drug that will cause a peaceful death?
- What about a young adult with severe brain damage who is living in a persistent vegetative state? Do family members wait for an unlikely recovery or remove life support?
- What about a middle-aged man diagnosed with an untreatable and fatal form of cancer that is severely weakening his body? What if he wants to end the suffering and his family approves of his decision?

Before deciding when or if euthanasia is morally acceptable, it is important to understand various relevant terms.

Euthanasia Terminology

Passive euthanasia	Intentionally withholding treatment to allow a patient to die
Active euthanasia	Intentionally killing a patient by lethal injection, smothering, or some other method
Extraordinary treatment	Surgery, medication, dialysis, oxygen, CPR, or any other treatment needed to help an unhealthy patient
Ordinary care	Food, water, and any other care people need regardless of their health
Voluntary euthanasia	A competent and completely informed patient freely requests or consents to euthanasia
Nonvoluntary euthanasia	An incompetent patient or one who has not given consent undergoes euthanasia
Involuntary euthanasia	Intentionally killing a patient against his or her will— considered murder

As indicated by the table, informed consent is required for voluntary euthanasia. Philosophers use the term *autonomy* when referring to the idea of informed consent. Actions are autonomous when they are intentional, understood, and chosen freely. Both Aristotle and Kant, for example, place great value in autonomy when making decisions.

Voluntary euthanasia is mostly illegal in the United States. However, some ethicists and activists campaign for the "right to die," arguing that it is morally unjustifiable for individuals to experience continuous and unnecessary suffering, particularly when it is due to terminal illness. Instead, "right-to- die" activists believe patients should not only have the right to refuse extraordinary treatment and reject efforts to extend their lives through artificial means, they should also be allowed to hire a medical professional to administer active euthanasia. This alternative is frequently referred to as "death with dignity," which implies that the patient is acting autonomously and that death prevents further degradation in quality of life. A common method of voluntary euthanasia is physician-assisted suicide, which currently can result in imprisonment and fines for the doctor in much of the country. This raises the question of whom the law is intended to protect if the victim of the crime is someone who has consented to it.

Economic Issues and Civil Rights

Economic Inequality

The distribution of wealth and resources both within the United States and around the world raises ethical issues about economic inequality. John Rawls asserted that economic inequality is justified only when it benefits everyone, such as to encourage people to be more productive. Rousseau believed that an excessive degree of inequality destroys freedom if wealthy citizens act as tyrants in a society.

Opponents of economic equality claim that diversity within a society is highly valuable and that people should have the freedom to keep what they have earned. They argue that economic redistribution, which refers to taking from those who have many resources and giving to those who have few resources, violates the rights of the individuals who acquired the resources in the first place.

Affirmative Action

Affirmative action refers to policies and programs that consider race, gender, or ethnicity for a range of purposes. A moderate type of affirmative action program might attempt to increase the diversity of applicants for a school or a job. For example, a university might include pictures in its admissions brochures that show people of different races and ethnic backgrounds to convey the idea that the campus is diverse. Preferential treatment is a controversial method of implementing affirmative action that involves promoting certain college or job applicants based primarily on their race, gender, or ethnicity. Preferential treatment often assigns less importance to factors such as standardized tests, as some studies show that they do not assess intelligence or probability of academic success in a consistent manner across social groups.

Affirmative action advocates claim that the preferential treatment for African Americans is justified because historical forms of oppression and discrimination, such as slavery and "separate but equal" segregation laws, produced societal disadvantages and inequalities that still exist today. Affirmative action is thus proposed as a way to "level the playing field" and provide minorities with opportunities now that were not available to them in the past. It is also proposed as a remedy for institutional racism, a term some use to describe prejudice in systems such as education, criminal justice, housing, and the economy. Advocates of affirmative action often assert that those institutions both actively and passively discriminate against minorities and thus present obstacles to success. To illustrate that point, they refer to statistics that show that African Americans are disproportionately likely to be imprisoned for minor offenses, face challenges in securing loans for homes and businesses, and are less likely to graduate from high school or attend college.

Critics of affirmative action argue that the economic and social circumstances of minorities are better now than they have ever been in the past, and that America's legal, political, and social structures are designed to be fair for everyone. For example, critics point to laws such as the Fair Housing Act and the Civil Rights Act, which prohibit discrimination based on race, color, religion, nationality, and familial status.

Crime and Punishment

The majority of Americans view crime reduction as an important objective, but the best method of reducing crime remains debatable. Some people argue that the threat of punishment deters criminal activity, while others assert that focusing on societal problems like alcoholism, poverty, and drug abuse deters crime. However, giving attention to the causes of crime will most likely not eliminate all criminal activity. Moreover, most people believe that criminals should be punished. In general, punishment should match the crime, but such a concept raises many questions: How long should prison sentences be? What should the conditions in prison be like?

How should youthful offenders be punished? What about criminals with mental disabilities?

Three general types of punishment are available within the American criminal justice system:

1. *Disablement*: placing a convicted criminal in prison or executing a criminal
2. *Deterrence*: when punishment is considered as a consequence, it can prevent (or deter) an individual from committing a crime.
3. *Rehabilitation*: prisoners spend time earning an education or learning a trade that can be used once released from prison to avoid the lure of criminal activity

Capital punishment is a controversial topic in the United States. Supporters of the death penalty assert that the threat of capital punishment is more effective than the threat of imprisonment for potential murderers. Advocates claim that capital punishment is morally acceptable because it protects society from the worst criminals. Additional arguments in favor of capital punishment include the idea that murderers deserve to die and that the death penalty provides closure for victims' families.

In contrast, opponents of capital punishment claim that life imprisonment satisfactorily removes a murderer from society. They also assert that imprisonment is just as effective in deterring crime as the death penalty. According to research studies, the likelihood of apprehension, conviction, and punishment is a more significant deterrent than the severity of the punishment when people decide whether to commit crimes. Mistakes made in the criminal justice system and questions regarding discrimination are issues continually raised in the death penalty debate as well. In 1972, the Supreme Court instituted a moratorium on capital punishment nationwide, after deciding that it constituted cruel and unusual punishment and was frequently imposed unfairly. The moratorium was later lifted, and now individual states can decide whether the death penalty is legal or not.

Quality of life for inmates is also a heavily debated topic in America. Many ethicists and lawmakers argue that prisons should be reformed to be more humane and less crowded with minor offenders. There are historical precedents for this modern discourse of prison reform. In the eighteenth and nineteenth centuries, the philosopher Jeremy Bentham analyzed contemporary methods of punishment and theorized that it would be more worthwhile to educate inmates and provide them with moral instruction than it would be to isolate and torture them, as was common at the time. An educated and repentant criminal, he argued, could eventually become a contributing member of society. He devised a model prison called the Panopticon that promoted civility, order, and virtue through a practice of constant surveillance.

Today, prison reform advocates take a similar position, arguing that while heinous crimes cannot go unpunished, many criminals, even violent ones, are capable of rehabilitation and reentry into society. Many advocates campaign to end solitary confinement, which is seen as a form of cruel and unusual punishment, as well as to curb abuse of inmates by prison officers. Reducing inmate populations is also a major goal of prison reform. One proposed means of achieving that is eliminating mandatory minimum sentences—for example, imposing a mandatory five-year sentence for drug trafficking. Supporters of mandatory minimum sentences, on the other hand, say that such laws are an appropriate way to ensure equal application of the law, as in the past, prison sentences may have been administered in a discriminatory fashion.

War and Peace

Wars have been fought for thousands of years and continue in modern society. War occurs for a variety of reasons—defending from attack, protecting natural resources, acquiring territory, and settling disputes. The way in which militaries fight wars varies as well and may include bombings, assassinations, and biological weapons. There are two primary questions related to the morality of war that must be asked by government leaders, soldiers, and regular citizens:

1. When is it morally acceptable to engage in war?
2. What are the moral limits, if any, during a war?

Peace refers to the absence of fighting, but non-warring conditions can vary. Peace occurred at the end of the U.S. Civil War when more than 600,000 soldiers lay dead. Peace existed between the United States and the Soviet Union during the Cold War, although weapons on both sides were ready to go at any moment. Peace occurs at times between Israel and the Palestinians, but it is always tenuous.

While many people take the view that peace requires preparation for war, pacifists believe war is never morally acceptable or justified. Pacifists think that war is an immoral way to achieve any goal and that war is ineffective because violence leads to more violence. Some pacifists cite the Hebrew Bible and the New Testament in protest of war. Other pacifists argue against war on pragmatic rather than moral or religious grounds and contend that there are more practical and effective ways, such as diplomacy, to resolve conflicts between nations and peoples.

Just War theory considers both the ethical and historical aspects of war. A war is justified under this theory if it meets certain criteria:

1. It is declared by a competent authority.
2. It is fought for a just cause.
3. It is fought with the right intentions.
4. It is appropriate for the provocation.
5. It is used as a last resort.
6. There is a reasonable chance for success.

The Just War tradition stems from the Roman Catholic Church, and St. Thomas Aquinas is linked to the first three justifications.

Life- and Human-Centered Ethics

Environmental Ethics

Environmental ethics is a relatively new field of philosophy that focuses on human responsibility to nature. Protecting the natural environment is viewed as both practical and ethical for the future of humanity.

Much has been said in recent years about environmental threats such as global climate change, air pollution, and energy consumption. The following list indicates the major environmental issues facing America and the rest of the world:

- Air pollution
- Deforestation
- Energy consumption
- Global climate change
- Ozone depletion
- Population growth
- Water pollution
- Wilderness preservation

While everyone generally agrees on the causes of some environmental concerns, such as water pollution, other issues are highly debatable. For example, some scientists blame the burning of fossil fuels for global climate change, while other experts attribute climate change to natural planetary and solar fluctuations. Energy consumption is another topic that triggers debate. Should the United States focus on developing alternative energy sources, or should it drill for oil where it is known to exist? Not only do environmental concerns raise ethical questions, but they raise issues about government policies as well.

Within ethical debates about the environment, some take the position that humans are equal to all other parts of nature, and others express a human-centered perspective, often referred to as *anthropocentrism*. The twentieth-century philosopher and naturalist Arne Naess developed an ethical theory known as "deep ecology." Naess argued that human beings are interconnected with all other forms of life on Earth and need to undergo a change of moral, philosophical, and political perspective in order to prevent impending ecological disaster. Naess was critical of capitalism and modern technological advances that endangered ecosystems and animal habitats.

Naess devised this eight-point platform for the **deep ecology movement:**

1. All life has value in itself, independent of its usefulness to humans.
2. Richness and diversity contribute to life's well-being and have value in themselves.
3. Humans have no right to reduce this richness and diversity except to satisfy vital needs in a responsible way.
4. The impact of humans in the world is excessive and rapidly getting worse.
5. Human lifestyles and population are key elements of this impact.
6. The diversity of life, including cultures, can flourish only with reduced human impact.
7. Basic ideological, political, economic, and technological structures must therefore change.
8. Those who accept the foregoing points have an obligation to participate in implementing the necessary changes and to do so peacefully and democratically.

Anthropocentrism is not necessarily opposed to the values of deep ecology. Ethicists who take this position often agree with environmentalists like Naess that the beauty, stability, and integrity of our natural resources should be maintained. However, rather than considering all living organisms as inherently equal in value, anthropocentric theorists contend that humans do have significant advantages over other forms of life; for example, higher intellectual ability and a refined sense of morality. In some cases, thus, anthropocentrism allows for the prioritization of human needs over other forms of life.

Human Rights

Since Ancient Greek civilization, philosophers have debated what inherent rights and privileges individuals are born with or are endowed with by God or nature. For much of recorded history, many of these rights have belonged only to certain categories of people, such as men or individuals with wealth, a certain skin color, or noble lineage. More recently, however, the concept of universal human rights has become more widely acknowledged, celebrated, and legally enforced. Around the world, women, minorities, and other groups that have historically been marginalized now have the right to vote, own property, freely express opinions, and marry. However, there remain considerable inequalities, and in many nations, individuals still live in slavery or under repressive governments.

The **Universal Declaration of Human Rights (UDHR)** was one of the first efforts to define and protect human rights in the past century. The United Nations issued the UDHR in 1948, claiming that the two world wars demonstrated an urgent need to protect individual freedoms and end widespread oppression. The UDHR outlines more than thirty fundamental rights that belong to everyone, irrespective of race, color, sex, language, religion, political opinion, national origin, or other status. These include the following:

- "No one shall be subjected to arbitrary arrest, detention, or exile."
- "Everyone has the right to a nationality."
- "Everyone has the right to a standard of living adequate for the health and well-being of himself and of his family."
- "Everyone, without any discrimination, has the right to equal pay for equal work."
- "Everyone has the right to education."

The UDHR has inspired many sovereign nations to adopt laws that preserve these rights for its citizens. While the UDHR is not legally binding anywhere in the world, there are some judicial systems, such as the International Criminal Court, which prosecute and punish individuals for genocide and other violations of human rights.

There is an active debate about whether women, LGBT (lesbian, gay, bisexual, and transgender) individuals, minorities, children, and other social groups deserve special considerations under the law, or whether general recognition of human rights sufficiently protects all members of society.

Biomedical Ethics

Due to advances in medical technology, such as vaccinations, organ transplants, and cancer treatment, humans are living longer than ever before. Despite these advances, however, we are still ultimately mortal and vulnerable to disease, pain, and suffering. As it has been throughout history, we entrust experts and professionals to help us live healthy and fulfilling lives, which raises many ethical questions.

Physicians, nurses, emergency medical technicians, insurance companies, and other health care providers make decisions every day about how to properly preserve patients' health and when to potentially allow a patient to die or experience extreme pain. How long is it necessary to prolong life for a mortally wounded, terminally ill, or comatose patient? Who receives medical treatment when resources are scarce, such as during a disease outbreak or war? Who is entitled to know confidential details about another person's medical history? Can a physician fulfill a patient's wishes to end his or her life through euthanasia?

These questions, and many others, are addressed in biomedical ethics, a field that can be traced back to Hippocrates. The fifth-century BCE Greek physician composed the **"Hippocratic Oath,"** to which many medical professionals still adhere today. The oath compels physicians to take every possible measure to ensure patients' health, to avoid harming patients, to respect patients' privacy, and to treat patients with dignity and respect. Yet this historic document also has many detractors who believe that profound and sweeping changes in technology, politics, and culture, as well as increasing specialization in medical fields, has made the oath outdated. Some of the questions raised by detractors include: Should physicians with specialties as different as dermatology and brain surgery have to swear to the same oath? In an era in which abortion is widely legal, how do we interpret the provision to "do no harm"? Should violating the oath carry any penalties?

More recently, the ethicists Tom Beauchamp and James Childress outlined four broad principles of biomedical ethics, which are frequently applied by medical professionals facing difficult decisions in the course of everyday treatment.

1. Autonomy: Every individual has the right to make his or her own choices. For example, a patient can sign a "do not resuscitate" form, which indicates a personal decision to refuse extraordinary care in the event of a medical emergency.

2. Beneficence: Medical professionals should act with the best interests of the patient in mind. Applying this principle, a physician might prescribe antibiotics to a patient suffering from a bacterial infection.

3. Justice: Medical services and resources should be distributed in a way that is fair. Applying this principle, during a disease outbreak, a team of doctors might perform "triage"—that is, decide which individuals or groups have the most urgent needs—and provide vaccinations to patients with the weakest immune systems.

4. Non-maleficence: Medical professionals should not intentionally cause harm to a patient. Applying this principle, a dental surgeon might administer anesthesia to a patient undergoing a root canal, so as to not cause excessive and unnecessary pain during the surgery.

In the United States, these ethical principles are often enforced through laws and regulations, for example, the 1996 Health Insurance Portability and Accountability Act (HIPAA). The act establishes guidelines for maintaining the privacy and security of information about patients' health. For example, the law disallows most employers from soliciting information about employees' and job applicants' medical history, in order to prevent discrimination.

Other topics of concern to biomedical ethicists include cloning, stem cell research, and human genetic engineering. Modern technology allows for many sophisticated and potentially dangerous decisions to be made about human life. For example, scientists now know the sequence and purpose of the entire human genome, which includes more than 20,000 individual genes that determine traits ranging from eye color to likelihood of contracting certain diseases. The availability of such information, combined with the practice of genetic screening, could eventually lead to discrimination against individuals applying for jobs or college, who have allegedly "inferior" innate characteristics. It is also conceivable that someday, attempts could be made to genetically engineer more "perfect" humans without handicaps or physical abnormalities or with only one skin color or body size—a widely condemned practice known as eugenics.

Should the possibility that research may eventually be used for dangerous or inhumane ends prevent modern scientists from making great advances? Must scientists weigh ethical dilemmas of the future against the possibility of curing cancer or AIDS today? The complexity and evolving challenges posed by biomedical ethics are no doubt why medical organizations are among the top employers of professional ethicists in the world today.

SUMMING IT UP

- **Ethics** refers to the academic discipline of analyzing morality. Reasoning, rules, and logic form the basis of ethical philosophy.
- **Cosmology** is the study of the physical world—what it is made of and how it works.
- **Cosmogony** is the study of the origin of the universe—how it came into existence.
- **Pythagoras**, one of the most notable pre-Socratic philosophers, was also a mathematician and a cosmologist. No writings of his exist, but evidence shows his philosophy was based on beliefs in the magic of numbers and reincarnation.
- The **Sophists** were traveling teachers who lectured about various topics for fees. Protagoras, a well-respected Sophist, is best known for stating, "Man is the measure of all things," suggesting that people rather than nature determine behavior.
- **Thucydides**, a Greek historian, wrote *The History of the Peloponnesian War* as a report of the battle between Athens and Sparta (431–404 BCE). He objectively presented factual events and questioned the ethics of war.
- **Socrates** lived in Athens during the fifth century BCE. An outspoken critic of the Sophists, and Athenian politics and religious institutions, he believed that virtue equaled knowledge and that a person who is knowledgeable about morality will behave with morality.
- Socrates' most famous student, **Plato**, was a philosopher and mathematician. After Socrates' death, Plato established the Academy in 387 BCE. His most influential work, *The Republic*, examines whether it is always better to be just than unjust.
- **Aristotle**, a renowned student of Plato's Academy, was a philosopher and an authority on nearly every subject. Aristotle believed everything had a purpose and change is both necessary and natural.
- **Stoicism** is a philosophy based on the idea that absolute law rules the universe and that humans cannot change fate. Epictetus was one of the most prominent Stoics of the second century AD.
- Around 300 BCE, hedonism or **Epicureanism** emerged under the guidance of Epicurus, who asserted that happiness was the purpose of life and that the universe was created by an accidental collision of atoms rather than by Greek gods.
- The **Bible** has been the most popular tool for teaching morality in the Western world and serves as the center point for Judeo-Christian ethics. While these ethics have had a major influence on law and customs in the United

States, the Constitution implies that there should ultimately be a separation of church and state.

- **The major world religions include Christianity, Judaism, Islam, Hinduism, and Buddhism.** Judaism, Christianity, and Islam are **monotheistic religions**—they believe in only one god rather than in multiple gods. Hinduism and Buddhism share the concepts of karma and dharma.
- **Natural law theories** are based on the idea that the moral standards guiding human behavior originate in human nature and the universe and that deviating from the norm is immoral, sinful, evil, and harmful. Many medieval philosophers adopted natural law theories to explain the relationship between God and man, including St. Thomas Aquinas, who believed that faith and reason could exist together.
- **Social contract theory** refers to the idea that the right to rule and the obligation to obey are based upon an agreement, a moral code, between an individual and society. Thomas Hobbes, John Locke, and Jean-Jacques Rousseau wrote about social contract theory during the seventeenth and eighteenth centuries.
- **John Rawls** and **Robert Nozick**, twentieth-century American philosophers, were known for their ideas regarding political philosophy.
- **Transcendental idealism**, a concept most often associated with eighteenth-century German philosophers, such as **Immanuel Kant**, contends that appearances should be viewed only as representations and not as things themselves—that both the mind and understanding create reality.
- **Adam Smith**, an early theorist of capitalism, proposed that the common good of society advances when individuals focus on benefiting themselves, a concept related to the theory of **moral egoism.**
- **Ayn Rand**, twentieth-century Russian philosopher and moral egoist, asserted that pursuing self-interests and personal happiness are "the highest moral purpose" of life.
- **Utilitarianism** (consequentialism) is the theory that actions are morally acceptable if good consequences outweigh bad consequences. Utilitarian philosophers include **Jeremy Bentham** and **John Stuart Mill.**
- **Feminism** is the philosophical and political discourse aimed at exposing, analyzing, and addressing gender inequality. Feminist philosophy emerged in the 1960s.
- Psychologist **Carol Gilligan** asserts that women and men have different approaches to making moral decisions—men focus on applying rules and minimizing emotions, and women appeal to emotions such as sympathy, love, and concern.

- Philosopher **Nel Noddings** studies the concept of **ethics of care**, focusing on the origins of care within the home, such as parent-child relationships.
- **Determinism** is the philosophical theory that past events, combined with the laws of nature, make certain outcomes inevitable. **Compatibilism** is the theory that behaviors and decisions are heavily influenced by natural forces, but that individuals can exercise free will as well.
- **Relativism** is the philosophical theory that there is no absolute moral truth and, instead, ethics and values are circumstantial or context-specific; what is moral here and now may not be moral somewhere else or in the future. **Subjectivism** is the theory that all ethical statements are an expression of personal perception rather than an indicator of absolute, verifiable truth.
- Current **ethical issues** include morality and sexuality, abortion, suicide, euthanasia, economic inequality, affirmative action, crime and punishment, war and peace, environmentalism, and biomedical ethics.

Chapter 4

Ethics In America Post-Test

POST-TEST ANSWER SHEET

1. Ⓐ Ⓑ Ⓒ Ⓓ	18. Ⓐ Ⓑ Ⓒ Ⓓ	35. Ⓐ Ⓑ Ⓒ Ⓓ
2. Ⓐ Ⓑ Ⓒ Ⓓ	19. Ⓐ Ⓑ Ⓒ Ⓓ	36. Ⓐ Ⓑ Ⓒ Ⓓ
3. Ⓐ Ⓑ Ⓒ Ⓓ	20. Ⓐ Ⓑ Ⓒ Ⓓ	37. Ⓐ Ⓑ Ⓒ Ⓓ
4. Ⓐ Ⓑ Ⓒ Ⓓ	21. Ⓐ Ⓑ Ⓒ Ⓓ	38. Ⓐ Ⓑ Ⓒ Ⓓ
5. Ⓐ Ⓑ Ⓒ Ⓓ	22. Ⓐ Ⓑ Ⓒ Ⓓ	39. Ⓐ Ⓑ Ⓒ Ⓓ
6. Ⓐ Ⓑ Ⓒ Ⓓ	23. Ⓐ Ⓑ Ⓒ Ⓓ	40. Ⓐ Ⓑ Ⓒ Ⓓ
7. Ⓐ Ⓑ Ⓒ Ⓓ	24. Ⓐ Ⓑ Ⓒ Ⓓ	41. Ⓐ Ⓑ Ⓒ Ⓓ
8. Ⓐ Ⓑ Ⓒ Ⓓ	25. Ⓐ Ⓑ Ⓒ Ⓓ	42. Ⓐ Ⓑ Ⓒ Ⓓ
9. Ⓐ Ⓑ Ⓒ Ⓓ	26. Ⓐ Ⓑ Ⓒ Ⓓ	43. Ⓐ Ⓑ Ⓒ Ⓓ
10. Ⓐ Ⓑ Ⓒ Ⓓ	27. Ⓐ Ⓑ Ⓒ Ⓓ	44. Ⓐ Ⓑ Ⓒ Ⓓ
11. Ⓐ Ⓑ Ⓒ Ⓓ	28. Ⓐ Ⓑ Ⓒ Ⓓ	45. Ⓐ Ⓑ Ⓒ Ⓓ
12. Ⓐ Ⓑ Ⓒ Ⓓ	29. Ⓐ Ⓑ Ⓒ Ⓓ	46. Ⓐ Ⓑ Ⓒ Ⓓ
13. Ⓐ Ⓑ Ⓒ Ⓓ	30. Ⓐ Ⓑ Ⓒ Ⓓ	47. Ⓐ Ⓑ Ⓒ Ⓓ
14. Ⓐ Ⓑ Ⓒ Ⓓ	31. Ⓐ Ⓑ Ⓒ Ⓓ	48. Ⓐ Ⓑ Ⓒ Ⓓ
15. Ⓐ Ⓑ Ⓒ Ⓓ	32. Ⓐ Ⓑ Ⓒ Ⓓ	49. Ⓐ Ⓑ Ⓒ Ⓓ
16. Ⓐ Ⓑ Ⓒ Ⓓ	33. Ⓐ Ⓑ Ⓒ Ⓓ	50. Ⓐ Ⓑ Ⓒ Ⓓ
17. Ⓐ Ⓑ Ⓒ Ⓓ	34. Ⓐ Ⓑ Ⓒ Ⓓ	51. Ⓐ Ⓑ Ⓒ Ⓓ

52. Ⓐ Ⓑ Ⓒ Ⓓ   55. Ⓐ Ⓑ Ⓒ Ⓓ   58. Ⓐ Ⓑ Ⓒ Ⓓ

53. Ⓐ Ⓑ Ⓒ Ⓓ   56. Ⓐ Ⓑ Ⓒ Ⓓ   59. Ⓐ Ⓑ Ⓒ Ⓓ

54. Ⓐ Ⓑ Ⓒ Ⓓ   57. Ⓐ Ⓑ Ⓒ Ⓓ   60. Ⓐ Ⓑ Ⓒ Ⓓ

ETHICS IN AMERICA POST-TEST

Directions: Carefully read each of the following 60 questions. Choose the best answer to each question and fill in the corresponding circle on the answer sheet. The Answer Key and Explanations can be found following this post-test.

1. The U.S. Supreme Court suspended the death penalty in 1972, because it

    A. violated the principles of federalism.
    B. constituted cruel and unusual punishment.
    C. violated the right to a fair trial.
    D. constituted murder.

2. Which of these is a limitation of the Universal Declaration of Human Rights?

    A. is not legally binding in any country.
    B. It was never adopted by the United Nations.
    C. It has had no influence on laws around the world.
    D. It does not renounce slavery.

3. For a follower of Kant, the ethical evaluation of a decision to commit adultery depends on whether

    A. the adulterer is a Christian.
    B. adultery is a reasonable action.
    C. the adulterer will be happy.
    D. adultery is moral for everyone.

4. According to which of the following is it immoral to engage in war?

    A. Smith, because war serves no self-interests
    B. Gandhi, because war is never justified
    C. Rawls, because war destroys freedom
    D. Mill, because war is irrational

5. Which of these businesses would a follower of Arne Naess most likely support?

A. One that maximized profits
B. One that used technology to make work more efficient
C. One that undertook "green" or sustainability initiatives
D. One that resisted paying income taxes

6. The idea that all events occur because of previous actions and the laws of nature is

A. rationalism.
B. existentialism.
C. determinism.
D. scholasticism.

7. Which of the following is equivalent to murder in most cases?

A. Passive euthanasia
B. Involuntary euthanasia
C. Active euthanasia
D. Nonvoluntary euthanasia

8. According to Rawls, in which of the following situations is economic inequality ethical and justified?

A. When citizens are required to share resources
B. When the wealthy rule government offices
C. When citizens need to be more productive
D. When society has become too diverse

9. Plato uses the Allegory of the Cave to illustrate which of the following concepts?

A. The world can only be understood intellectually.
B. Happiness can be attained through physical experiences.
C. The world can only be understood through the senses.
D. Courage and morality are necessary in difficult situations.

10. The ethics of Judaism are based on the teachings of

A. the Old Testament.
B. Jesus Christ.
C. Mohammed.
D. the New Testament.

11. Which of these circumstances best describes a direct conflict between beneficence and non-maleficence?

    A. A hospital bans smoking in the lobby.
    B. A patient confides to his physician that he is gay.
    C. A promising experimental cancer treatment causes severe side effects.
    D. A patient asks her family to make medical decisions on her behalf.

12. According to which of the following philosophies is premarital sex most likely immoral?

    A. Moral egoism, because increasing knowledge is the most important goal
    B. Hedonism, because the gods will disapprove
    C. Transcendental idealism, because logical thinking equals happiness
    D. Stoicism, because self-control is virtuous

13. Determinism poses a challenge to the idea of moral responsibility in suggesting that

    A. God forgives immoral actions after repentance.
    B. individuals' actions are caused by natural forces.
    C. no one can objectively judge others' morality.
    D. all actions that benefit oneself are moral.

14. The statement "To each according to need" is an example of the principles of

    A. retributive justice.
    B. economic rationalism.
    C. distributive justice.
    D. social virtue.

15. According to which of the following philosophers is economic equality moral?

    A. Smith, because the purpose of society is to share wealth
    B. Rand, because helping others is the greatest moral purpose
    C. Bentham, because individual happiness is the purpose of life
    D. Rousseau, because excessive inequality undermines freedom

16. What was the Supreme Court's ruling in the 1973 case
    Roe v. Wade?

    A. Most abortion procedures are legal, because privacy is a right.
    B. All abortion procedures are legal, including during the third
    trimester.
    C. All abortion procedures are illegal, because they are a form of
    euthanasia.
    D. Abortion is legal only through the first four weeks of
    pregnancy.

17. What do "right-to-die" activists want to legalize?

    A. Capital punishment
    B. Abortion
    C. Voluntary euthanasia
    D. Involuntary euthanasia

18. A lawmaker who agreed with Mill's thesis in *The Subjugation of
    Women* would likely vote for a bill that

    A. establishes college scholarships for women.
    B. overturns women's suffrage.
    C. legalizes polygamy for certain religious groups.
    D. allows a man to take his ex-wife's property in a divorce.

19. According to Smith, which of the following is the best way to find
    happiness in life?

    A. Share resources with others.
    B. Accept life the way it is.
    C. Refrain from showing emotion.
    D. Focus on personal interests.

20. According to Locke, what should citizens do when ruled by an
    unjust political authority?

    A. Resist and revolt.
    B. Search for answers.
    C. Submit to authority.
    D. Accept the fate of nature.

21. An advocate for affirmative action would agree that

A. standardized testing is the best indicator of intellectual ability.
B. universities should enforce moral virtues.
C. minority students are intellectually superior.
D. "separate but equal" laws have left a lasting impact on society.

22. "Deep ecology" is a form of environmental ethics that

A. is anthropocentric.
B. values animal and plant life over human life.
C. is compatible with the current state of industrial capitalism.
D. critiques modern patterns of consumption and development.

23. Sophism most likely arose in Ancient Greece because of the

A. condemnation of Socrates.
B. war between Athens and Sparta.
C. opening of the Athens Academy.
D. growing democratic system.

24. For an Epicurean, the ethical evaluation of a decision to perform euthanasia will depend on whether the action will

A. adhere to the natural laws of the world.
B. avoid pain and increase happiness.
C. maximize utility for everyone.
D. lead to retribution from the gods.

25. A hospital managing vaccines during a disease outbreak will be most concerned about which principle of biomedical ethics?

A. Autonomy
B. Orthodoxy
C. Referral
D. Justice

26. The idea that the universe is morally neutral is a concept related to

A. feminist ethics.
B. Indian philosophy.
C. natural law theories.
D. social contract theories.

27. A "do not resuscitate" form, signed by a competent patient, constitutes a rejection of

A. active euthanasia.
B. autonomy.
C. extraordinary treatment.
D. ordinary care.

28. Which of the following writings develops the concept of the general will in society?

A. *Discourse on Political Economy* by Rousseau
B. *A Theory of Justice* by Rawls
C. *The Wealth of Nations* by Smith
D. *On Liberty* by Mill

29. Advocates of prison reform are most critical of what kind of punishment?

A. Disablement
B. Deterrence
C. Rehabilitation
D. Probation

30. Which of these positions would a pragmatic pacifist most strongly support?

A. All violence is inherently immoral.
B. Diplomacy is more effective than warfare.
C. Wars that depose brutal dictators can be justified.
D. Wars that result in the spread of democracy can be justified.

31. Which statement would most likely convince a follower of John Rawls to support an affirmative action policy?

A. It recognizes everyone's right to equal opportunity.
B. It reconciles past societal injustices.
C. It was approved by the democratically elected student government.
D. It will benefit you personally.

32. Which of the following would most likely disagree with the concept of redistributing wealth?

A. Hobbes, because it is an irrational concept
B. Rand, because of the personal sacrifices required
C. Rawls, because of the burden placed on some citizens
D. Kant, because of an individual's right to property

33. For a Kantian, the ethical evaluation of capital punishment mostly depends on

A. natural and civil laws.
B. assessing consequences.
C. long-term societal benefits.
D. developing a universal law.

34. Which of the following statements best explains ethical relativism?

A. Knowledge is derived from observations.
B. Every point of view is equally valid.
C. Reality consists of one substance.
D. Nothing in life actually matters.

35. In which way are determinism and deep ecology philosophically compatible?

A. Both agree that humans determine their own destinies.
B. Both agree that humans have dominion over nature.
C. Both agree that human life is interconnected with nature.
D. Both agree that humans cannot change their behavior.

36. All of the following are assertions made by Locke in *Two Treatises of Government* EXCEPT:

A. People have the right to own property.
B. People have the right to form militias.
C. People have the right to make their own choices.
D. People have the right to live without being harmed by others.

37. According to Rousseau, which of the following best explains why people commit crimes?

    A. Society has corrupted them.
    B. People are innately selfish.
    C. People lack moral knowledge.
    D. Natural laws encourage immorality.

38. Which of the following concepts are most closely associated with Hinduism and Buddhism?

    A. Love and salvation
    B. Laws and responsibilities
    C. Obedience and remorse
    D. Actions and duties

39. In the United States, what do HIPAA standards enforce?

    A. Affirmative action policies for hospitals
    B. Patient privacy
    C. Universal healthcare
    D. Nondiscrimination for preexisting conditions

40. According to Socrates, a man who robs a store at gunpoint is most likely

    A. acting out of personal freedom.
    B. immoral because he wants to be.
    C. behaving in the way nature intended.
    D. immoral because he lacks knowledge.

41. Which of the following best describes how Aquinas viewed nature?

    A. As a way to understand humanity
    B. As the ultimate source of life
    C. As an accidental collection of atoms
    D. As a way to draw close to God

42. Which of these phrases appears in the United States Constitution?

    A. "Separation of church and state"
    B. "No law respecting an establishment of religion"
    C. "Right to practice religion freely"
    D. "A national religion shall not be established."

43. According to which of the following philosophers is it immoral to tax people's income?

A. Rawls, because income taxes burden the wealthy
B. Smith, because income taxes discourage productivity
C. Nozick, because income tax is equivalent to forced labor
D. Noddings, because income tax does not create equity

44. According to Gilligan, when a woman faces a moral decision, she is most likely to

A. consider relationships.
B. minimize emotions.
C. apply standard rules.
D. assess ethical principles.

45. Subjectivism is the philosophical theory that

A. mental processes are not real.
B. human decisions are shaped by natural forces.
C. all citizens should be subject to the same legal standards.
D. all ethical statements are expressions of personal perception.

46. Which of the following is an example of triage?

A. Allowing women and children to board a lifeboat first
B. Performing elective cosmetic surgery
C. Medicating a patient against his consent
D. Prescribing chemotherapy to a latestage cancer patient

47. What did the U.S. Supreme Court legalize nationwide in the 2003 case, *Lawrence v. Texas*?

A. Contraception access
B. Same-sex sexual activity
C. Same-sex marriage
D. Pornography

48. Which of the following statements is a core belief of Aristotle?

A. Change is a man-made process.
B. Virtue is a transcendent quality.
C. Everything in life has a purpose.
D. Wisdom brings contentment.

49. Which of the following thinkers believed that humans cannot change fate because absolute law rules the universe?

A. Aquinas
B. Epictetus
C. Gandhi
D. Epicurus

50. A concept in which citizens act as legislators to determine collectively the laws of a society is known as

A. distributive justice.
B. social constructivism.
C. social contract theory.
D. general will.

51. Which of the following questions would most likely be asked by a utilitarian when making an ethical decision about an affirmative action policy?

A. Will an affirmative action policy benefit more people than it will harm?
B. How does an affirmative action policy correspond with natural laws?
C. Will an affirmative action policy allocate resources fairly and equally?
D. What do the majority of people think about an affirmative action policy?

52. Which of the following is a similarity between Kant's categorical imperatives and utilitarianism?

A. Both are methods for addressing societal immorality.
B. Both are ways to conceptualize people and decisions.
C. Both are preventive techniques for avoiding immorality.
D. Both are masculine approaches to ethical decision making.

53. Which of the following was the main criticism against the Sophists?

A. Their disbelief in the existence of the gods
B. Their support of the ideas presented by Socrates
C. Their domination in the Athenian government
D. Their reliance on persuasion instead of truth

54. Which of the following best describes Plato's ideal state in *The Republic*?

A. A society ruled by a political tyrant
B. A society based upon political justice
C. A society ruled by the general will
D. A society based upon a social contract

55. Which of the following is a type of moral excellence according to Aristotle?

A. Gentleness
B. Wisdom
C. Reason
D. Skill

56. Which of these statements best describes institutional racism?

A. Many people do not socialize outside of their own racial or ethnic groups.
B. A business owner overcharges minority customers.
C. Members of minority groups are frequently harassed by fellow citizens.
D. Racial biases are pervasive in education, criminal justice, and politics.

57. For a Hindu, the ethical evaluation of a decision to drill for oil in the Alaska wilderness depends on whether drilling

A. serves the self-interests of the citizens of Alaska.
B. causes minimal harm to citizens and the environment.
C. follows the desires of the majority of people in America.
D. reduces American dependency on foreign oil.

58. Which of the following is better known for his manner of teaching than his philosophy?

A. Plato
B. Aristotle
C. Socrates
D. Pythagoras

59. Which of the following thinkers provides the most pessimistic view of society?

    A. Hobbes, because he views society as a violent and insecure place

    B. Mill, because he views citizens as weak against the government

    C. Rousseau, because he views the monarchy as untrustworthy

    D. Locke, because he views citizens as immoral and irrational

60. Which of the following concepts is suggested in the works of Plato?

    A. Creating and appreciating beauty leads to contentment.

    B. Enlightened people receive their abilities from nature.

    C. Courage and morality lead societies out of darkness.

    D. Pursuing excellence helps attain peace in the world.

ANSWER KEY AND EXPLANATIONS

1. B	13. B	25. D	37. A	49. B
2. A	14. C	26. C	38. D	50. D
3. D	15. D	27. C	39. B	51. A
4. B	16. A	28. A	40. D	52. D
5. C	17. C	29. A	41. D	53. D
6. C	18. A	30. B	42. B	54. B
7. B	19. D	31. A	43. C	55. A
8. C	20. A	32. B	44. A	56. D
9. A	21. D	33. D	45. D	57. B
10. A	22. D	34. B	46. A	58. C
11. C	23. D	35. C	47. B	59. A
12. D	24. B	36. B	48. C	60. D

1. **The correct answer is B.** In the 1972 Supreme Court case *Furman v. Georgia*, the majority decided that the death penalty constituted cruel and unusual punishment, though the justices disagreed on why that was the case. Some argued that the penalty was imposed in an inconsistent manner, and others proposed that the capital punishment was in itself cruel, though not legally murder. Justices in the majority did not cite the Sixth Amendment, which guarantees the right to a fair trial, nor the Tenth Amendment, which reinforces the principle of federalism. Therefore, choices A, C, and D are incorrect.

2. **The correct answer is A.** The Universal Declaration of Human Rights (UDHR) is not legally binding anywhere in the world. Nevertheless, it was formally adopted by the United Nations in 1948, so choice B is incorrect. Many sovereign nations have adopted their own laws that are inspired by the UDHR's principles, so choice C is incorrect. Article 4 of the UDHR states that "No one shall be held in slavery or servitude," so choice D is incorrect.

3. **The correct answer is D.** The basis of morality for followers of Kant is whether the behavior is moral or immoral for all human beings according to universal moral laws. God, reason, and happiness are not important factors in ethical decisions based on Kant's philosophy, so choices A, B, and C are incorrect.

4. **The correct answer is B.** Gandhi was a pacifist, and pacifists believe that war is never moral or justified. According to pacifists, war is an immoral method to attain a goal in all situations. In many cases, war brings freedom and is a rational choice, so choices C and D are incorrect. Wars can be self-serving if they are a way to acquire land or other resources, so choice A is incorrect.

5. **The correct answer is C.** Arne Naess was one of the primary thinkers of the twentieth-century "deep ecology" movement, and he laid out ethical principles that centered on protecting natural resources and ecosystems. In particular, Naess sought to protect the soil and wrote that human thinking needed to undergo a paradigm shift—away from rampant technological development and profitmaking and toward respect for Earth. Choices A and B are thus incorrect. Tax resistance (choice D) is more closely aligned with the thinking of John Rawls.

6. **The correct answer is C.** The concept that all events occur because of previous actions and the laws of nature is determinism. Rationalism (choice A) is the idea that knowledge can be gained without having experiences. Existentialism (choice B) is the idea that people have to determine what life means. The philosophy of scholasticism (choice D) combines logic with a belief in God.

7. **The correct answer is B.** Involuntary euthanasia involves killing a patient against his or her will, which is considered murder in most cases. Passive euthanasia involves withholding treatment to allow a patient to die, while active euthanasia involves actively killing a patient, perhaps by lethal injection. Nonvoluntary euthanasia occurs when an incompetent patient undergoes euthanasia. Choices A, C, and D do not involve going against the will of the patient.

8. **The correct answer is C.** Rawls asserted that economic inequality is justified only when it benefits everyone, such as to encourage people to be more productive. Sharing resources would bring about equality, so choice A is incorrect. Rawls might argue that choice B is a reason for equality. The lack of diversity is an argument used against inequality, so choice D is incorrect.

9. The correct answer is A. The Allegory of the Cave illustrates the idea that the world experienced through the senses is not the real world. The world can truly be understood only on an intellectual level. Plato believed that happiness could be attained only through virtue, so choice B is incorrect.

10. The correct answer is A. The Old Testament, which is also known as the Hebrew Bible, is the ethical source for Judaism. Christians find ethical principles in both the Old Testament and the New Testament, which contains the teachings of Jesus Christ. Muslims turn to the words of the prophet Mohammed, so choice C is incorrect.

11. The correct answer is C. Beneficence is the biomedical ethics principle that physicians should take actions that are in the best interest of their patients' health and comfort. Non-maleficence is the biomedical ethics principle that physicians should not cause their patients any harm. A promising experimental cancer treatment would likely benefit a patient's health, but the severe side effects would likely cause some harm, thus bringing the two principles into conflict. Smoking bans both benefit and cause no harm to patients, so choice A is incorrect. Choices B and D primarily concern the principles of confidentiality and autonomy, so they are incorrect.

12. The correct answer is D. Stoicism finds self-control and reasoning the greatest virtues, and premarital sex most likely shows a lack of self-control. Stoics also advocated experiencing a passionless life. Moral egoism (choice A) focuses on self-interests, which may or may not be gained through premarital sex. Hedonists approved of anything pleasurable, so choice B is incorrect. Choice C is incorrect.

13. **The correct answer is B.** Moral responsibility presumes that individuals can exercise free will and choose between right and wrong. It would thus be difficult to hold an individual responsible for a crime or other offense if, as determinism suggests, all of our actions and decisions are predetermined by natural forces that we cannot control. Subjectivism suggests that no one can objectively judge others' morality, so choice C is incorrect. Moral egoism suggests that actions that benefit oneself are moral, so choice D is incorrect. Choice A is incorrect.

14. **The correct answer is C.** The statement "To each according to need" is an example of the principles of distributive justice. Distributive justice refers to the appropriate way of allocating benefits and obligations ina society. Retributive justice refers to what type of punishment is appropriate for a crime. Choices B and D are incorrect.

15. **The correct answer is D.** Rousseau believed that an excessive degree of inequality destroys freedom if wealthy citizens act as tyrants in a society. Smith and Rand advocated moral egoism and the protection of personal rather than societal interests, making choices A and B incorrect. Bentham believed people should improve happiness within society rather than increase personal happiness, so choice C is incorrect.

16. **The correct answer is A.** In a 7-2 decision, the U.S. Supreme Court ruled in *Roe v. Wade* that abortions during the first trimester of pregnancy were legal, because of the right to privacy guaranteed by the Fourteenth Amendment, and that second trimester abortions could be regulated somewhat, so choices C and D are incorrect. The Supreme Court left the legality of third trimester abortions to be decided by individual states, so choice B is incorrect.

17. **The correct answer is C.** "Right-to-die" activists campaign to legalize voluntary euthanasia, in which a mentally competent individual consents to being assisted in ending his or her life by a doctor or third party through an active or passive method of euthanasia. They also campaign to make euthanasia and suicide more societally acceptable practices, especially for terminally ill patients. "Right-to-die" activists do not support involuntary euthanasia, which is terminating the life of an individual without that individual's consent, so choice D is incorrect. Abortion (choice B) is typically advocated by "pro-choice" activists. Choice A is incorrect.

18. **The correct answer is A.** In *The Subjugation of Women*, the nineteenth-century British philosopher John Stuart Mill used a utilitarian approach to argue in favor of women's equality and their right to receive a good education. He supported a woman's right to vote, so choice B is incorrect. He also criticized the institution of marriage, and stated that marriage—if a woman freely consented to it—should be the union of two equal, independent partners, so choices C and D are incorrect.

19. **The correct answer is D.** Focusing on personal interests is the way to find happiness in life according to Smith. As a moral egoist, Smith asserted that the happiness of oneself is more important than the happiness of others. Choices B and C describe Stoics.

20. **The correct answer is A.** Locke asserted that people have the right to reject and resist any unjust political authority. Hobbes stated that failure to submit to an unjust ruler results in conflict. Stoics live their lives accepting what happens as fate.

21. **The correct answer is D.** One popular argument in favor of affirmative action is that injustices such as "separate but equal" (or "Jim Crow") laws have lasting impacts on society and continue to create disadvantages for African Americans and other minorities. Advocates for affirmative action usually argue that standardized testing is unfairly biased in favor of wealthier students who have access to tutors, so choice A is incorrect. Advocates do not argue that any type of student is intellectually superior, but rather that some have been unfairly marginalized because of who they are, so choice C is incorrect. Choice B is incorrect.

22. **The correct answer is D.** Deep ecology is the ethical theory that humankind is simply one element of a vast, interconnected ecosystem on Earth, and that all living organisms are equal in value and importance. It is thus highly critical of modern patterns of consumption and development, as well as modern industrial capitalism, which tend to destroy natural resources and endanger animals. Choices A, B, and C are incorrect.

23. **The correct answer is D.** The burgeoning democratic system in Ancient Greece most likely led to Sophism. The Sophists traveled around discussing politics and justice with the citizens of Athens, many of whom were required to participate in government. Socrates's condemnation by the Greek government (choice A), and Plato's opening of the Athens Academy (choice C) occurred after Sophism developed. The Peloponnesian War (choice B) was less influential than democracy on Sophism.

24. **The correct answer is B.** For an Epicurean, the ethical evaluation of a decision to perform euthanasia will depend on whether the action will avoid pain and increase happiness. Epicureans do not worry about retribution from the gods or nature, so choices A and D are incorrect. A utilitarian would be concerned about maximizing utility for everyone, so choice C is incorrect.

25. The correct answer is D. Justice is the principle of biomedical ethics that pertains to the fair and equitable distribution of scarce resources, such as vaccines. The principle of autonomy pertains to a patient's right to make decisions for himself or herself, so choice A is incorrect. Orthodoxy (choice B) and referral (choice C) are not principles of biomedical ethics, so they are incorrect.

26. The correct answer is C. The idea that the universe is morally neutral is a concept related to natural law theories. Natural law theories also assume that moral laws are part of nature. Social contract theories (choice D), feminist ethics (choice A), and Indian philosophies (choice B) are not based on assumptions regarding a morally neutral universe.

27. The correct answer is C. A competent patient who signs a "do not resuscitate" (DNR) form thereby requests that medical professionals *do not* attempt to administer extraordinary treatment such as CPR or defibrillation if his or her heart or breathing stops. A DNR form explicitly indicates consent and is an expression rather than a rejection of autonomy, so choice B is incorrect. Choices A and D are incorrect.

28. The correct answer is A. Rousseau develops the idea of the general will in society in *Discourse on Political Economy*. Under general will, citizens act as legislators to determine as a collective body the laws and legislation of society. Choices B, C, and D are incorrect.

29. The correct answer is A. Objectives of prison reform include reducing prison populations, making life in prison safer and more rehabilitative for inmates, and creating favorable conditions for inmates re-entering society on probation or parole. Prison reform advocates criticize minimum sentencing requirements as a factor that increases prison populations unnecessarily. Prison reformers tend to support deterrence (choice B), rehabilitation (choice C), and probation (choice D) as methods of addressing crime.

30. **The correct answer is B.** Pragmatic pacifists argue that violence and warfare are unnecessary and wrong, given that there are many other means, including diplomacy, to resolve disputes between nations and peoples. The idea that all violence is inherently immoral pertains to moral pacifism, so choice A is incorrect. Choices C and D pertain to Just War theory and are not pacifist principles.

31. **The correct answer is A.** John Rawls's first principle of justice is that "Each person is to have an equal right to the most extensive total system of equal basic liberties," so a follower of his would most likely be convinced by an appeal to equal rights. The reconciliation of past injustices is more so a concern of Robert Nozick, so choice B is incorrect. Democratic consensus is more so a concern of Immanuel Kant, so choice C is incorrect. Personal benefit is more so a concern of a moral egoist like Ayn Rand, so choice D is incorrect.

32. **The correct answer is B.** Rand would most likely disagree with the concept of redistributing wealth because she believed that doing anything for another person sacrificed personal happiness. In addition, she objected to what she viewed as the weak exploiting the strong. Rawls (choice C) was an advocate of distributive justice, so he would support wealth redistribution. Choices A and D are incorrect.

33. **The correct answer is D.** A follower of Kant makes an ethical evaluation of capital punishment based on the development of a universal law. In other words, capital punishment is moral if it is moral for all human beings. A Kantian would focus less on natural and civil laws (choice A), consequences (choice B), and long-term societal benefits (choice C).

34. **The correct answer is B.** According to ethical relativism, every point of view is equally valid, and different people have different behavior standards. Choice A refers to empiricism, and choice C refers to monism, a theory held by pre-Socratic philosophers. Choice D describes stoicism.

35. **The correct answer is C.** Hard determinism is the theory that our actions and decisions are completely controlled and predetermined by natural forces, and deep ecology is the theory that all living organisms on earth are connected and interdependent; therefore, they would agree that human life is interconnected with nature. Determinists do not believe in free will, so choices A and D are incorrect, and supporters of deep ecology believe that all organisms have equal claim to Earth, so choice B is incorrect.

36. **The correct answer is B.** In *Two Treatises of Government*, Locke asserts that people have three primary rights—life, liberty, and property. A modified version of these rights was included in the U.S. Declaration of Independence. The right to form militias is the Second Amendment to the U.S. Constitution, but it was not one of Locke's propositions.

37. **The correct answer is A.** Rousseau asserted that people are born innately good but that the greed and corruption in society corrupts them, which rules out choice B. The Greek philosophers believed that knowledge led to virtue, so choice C is incorrect. Rousseau did not blame natural laws for immorality, so choice D is incorrect.

38. **The correct answer is D.** Hinduism and Buddhism are most closely linked to actions and duties, or karma and dharma. *Karma* is the idea that a person's actions determine the future. *Dharma* refers to the righteous duties a person has toward people and gods. Choices A, B, and C are less associated with Buddhism and Hinduism.

39. **The correct answer is B.** HIPAA is the acronym for the Health Insurance Portability and Accountability Act, a law that regulates which entities can and cannot disclose private information about patients' medical histories. The Affordable Care Act, enacted later, guarantees that patients cannot be discriminated against by healthcare companies because of preexisting conditions, so choice D is incorrect. Choices A and C are incorrect.

40. **The correct answer is D.** According to Socrates, a man who robs a store at gunpoint is most likely immoral because he lacks knowledge. Socrates believed that virtue equaled knowledge, and wickedness resulted from ignorance. Choice B is incorrect because Socrates thought that people did not knowingly act immorally. Nature and personal freedom were less significant factors in morality than knowledge.

41. **The correct answer is D.** Aquinas viewed nature as a way to understand and draw close to God. Aquinas states that the laws discovered in nature stem from God. Aquinas attempted to understand the relationship between God and humanity, but he viewed nature as a way to understand God, not humans. Epicurus believed the universe was created by an accidental collision of atoms, so choice C is incorrect.

42. **The correct answer is B.** The First Amendment to the U.S. Constitution begins, "Congress shall make no law respecting an establishment of religion." Thomas Jefferson, as well as many legal scholars and Supreme Court justices, have interpreted this as establishing a "separation of church and state," but that phrase is not explicitly stated in the Constitution, so choice A is incorrect. Choices C and D express ideas that are in the First Amendment, but they are also not part of the actual text and are thus incorrect.

43. **The correct answer is C.** Nozick compared income taxes to forced labor. Rawls advocated distributive justice, so he would probably think taxes are moral. Smith wrote about capitalism in *The Wealth of Nations*, but he does not indicate that taxes discourage productivity. Noddings has focused her work on the ethics of care.

44. **The correct answer is A.** Gilligan found that women are more likely than men to consider responsibilities and relationships when making decisions. Men are more likely to minimize emotions and apply standard rules and principles when reaching a moral decision. Therefore, choices B, C, and D are incorrect.

45. **The correct answer is D.** Subjectivism is the philosophical theory that all statements about ethics are expressions of personal perception. Thus for a subjectivist, the expression "murder is wrong" is not a universal truth, but rather just the belief or common sense of the person expressing it. Choices A, B, and C are incorrect.

46. **The correct answer is A.** Triage, related to the biomedical ethics principle of justice, relates to the equitable distribution of resources, which often amounts to the decision of who lives and who dies. Allowing women and children to board a lifeboat first is just such a decision, as it allocates a scarce resource—space—to certain individuals but not others. Medicating a patient against his consent has more to do with autonomy than justice, so choice C is incorrect. Prescribing chemotherapy to a late-stage cancer patient is more relevant to the principles of beneficence and non-maleficence than justice, so choice D is incorrect. Choice B is also incorrect.

47. **The correct answer is B.** The majority decision in *Lawrence v. Texas* struck down sodomy laws, which had previously made same-sex sexual activity illegal in some states. Contraception access (choice A), same-sex marriage (choice C), and some types of pornography (choice D) were all legalized nationwide in other Supreme Court cases.

48. **The correct answer is C.** The idea that everything in life has a purpose was one of Aristotle's core beliefs. The other one is that change is both necessary and natural, so choice A is incorrect. Aristotle was extremely wise and learned, yet he continued to gain more knowledge, which means choice D is incorrect. Aristotle believed that virtue could be achieved through balance in life, so choice B is incorrect.

49. **The correct answer is B.** Stoics, such as Epictetus, believe that human beings cannot change fate because absolute law rules the universe. Epicurus was a hedonist who believed the universe was created by atoms colliding accidentally, so choice D is incorrect. Aquinas (choice A) was a Catholic priest who believed in God rather than fate. Hindus, such as Mohandas Gandhi (choice C) believe in many gods and karma rather than absolute law.

50. **The correct answer is D.** According to Rousseau's concept of general will, citizens act as legislators to determine as a collective body the laws and legislation of society. Rousseau is a social contract theorist, but the definition given is of general will rather than social contract theory.

51. **The correct answer is A.** A utilitarian views issues in terms of consequences and results. A utilitarian will most likely ask if an affirmative action policy will benefit more people than it will harm because the question addresses the benefits of the policy. Utilitarians are not concerned with natural laws, so choice B is incorrect. Choice C relates to a policy of distributive justice rather than utilitarianism. The opinion of the majority is insignificant to utilitarians, so choice D is incorrect.

52. **The correct answer is D.** Both Kant's categorical imperatives and utilitarianism are masculine approaches to ethical decision making. Carol Gilligan researched how men and women make moral decisions, and men typically focus on rules, as with Kant's method and utilitarianism. Choices A, B, and C are not similarities between the two philosophies.

53. **The correct answer is D.** Most of the criticism against the Sophists regarded their reliance on persuasion and manipulation instead of truth. The Sophists questioned the existence of the gods, but that was not a primary criticism against them. Socrates was the most vocal critic of the Sophists, so choice B is incorrect. The Sophists did not dominate the government (choice C), although they were influential.

54. **The correct answer is B.** In *The Republic,* society is based on political justice. Democracy, which is similar to Rousseau's general will, and tyranny are replaced, so choices A and C are incorrect. The idea of a social contract was not developed until the seventeenth century, so choice D is incorrect.

55. **The correct answer is A.** Gentleness is one of the moral virtues proposed by Aristotle in his book *Nicomachean Ethics.* Self-respect, bravery, truthfulness, and generosity are other moral virtues. Wisdom (choice B), reason (choice C), and skill (choice D) are examples of intellectual virtues.

56. **The correct answer is D.** The term *institutional racism* refers to how racial biases are prevalent in formal societal systems such as education, criminal justice, and politics. Self-selecting social groups (choice A), dishonest business practices (choice B), and harassment (choice C) can all involve racially biased sentiments or motivations, but they are different from institutional racism because they occur at the level of interpersonal relations rather than at the level of formal social and political institutions.

57. **The correct answer is B.** A Hindu would base a decision to drill for oil in the Alaska wilderness on the amount of harm it would cause. Hinduism advocates choosing actions that cause the least amount of harm, which in this case involves people and the environment. The opinion of the majority (choice C) and self-interests (choices A and D) would not be relevant factors in the decision-making process.

58. **The correct answer is C.** Socrates is better known for his method of teaching than for a specific philosophy. Socrates employed what is now known as the Socratic Method, which involves asking a student a series of questions in order to draw out the truth. Plato (choice A) and Aristotle (choice B) are both highly regarded for their philosophies. Pythagoras (choice D) was better known as a mathematician.

59. **The correct answer is A.** Hobbes holds the most pessimistic view of society, which he considers savage and full of conflict. He developed the social contract theory because he felt it was better for people to surrender some of their rights for the protection offered by a society. Rousseau (choice C) and Locke (choice D) were also social contract theorists, but they did not view the world as such a violent place like their peer. Mill (choice B) was a utilitarian who believed that the government had very limited moral authority over people.

60. **The correct answer is D.** Plato believed in pursuing personal excellence to achieve peace in a troubled world. During Plato's time, many people believed beauty equaled virtue, but Plato believed enlightenment gained from knowledge, not nature, was the key to virtue. Although the soldiers in Plato's *The Republic* are courageous and moral, the wise philosopher is the ruler, which means choice C is incorrect.

Like what you see? Get unlimited access to Peterson's full catalog of DSST practice tests, instructional videos, flashcards and more for **75% off the first month!** Go to **www.petersons.com/testprep/dsst** and use coupon code **DSST2020** at checkout. Offer expires July 1, 2021.

Printed in the USA
CPSIA information can be obtained
at www.ICGtesting.com
JSHW012045140824
68134JS00034B/3259